From Your Friends at **The MAILBOX®**

W9-CZL-613

Look 'n' Cook

Step-by-Step Recipes for Young Chefs

Project Manager:
Allison Ward

Writers:
Kimberli Carrier, Susan DeRiso, Sheri L. Green, Lynn C. Mode, Patricia Moeser,
Anita M. Ortiz, Sharla Park, Betty Silkunas, Margaret Southard, Dawn Spurck,
Ellen Van de Walle, Bonnie Vontz, Christina C. Yuhouse, Virginia Zeletzki

Editor:
Sherri Lynn Kuntz

Art Coordinator:
Kimberly Richard

Artists:
Pam Crane, Theresa Lewis Goode, Nick Greenwood, Sheila Krill,
Mary Lester, Kimberly Richard, Rebecca Saunders, Donna K. Teal

Cover Artists:
Nick Greenwood, Kimberly Richard

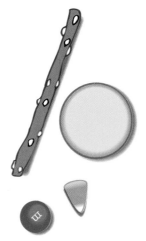

www.themailbox.com

©2001 by THE EDUCATION CENTER, INC.
All rights reserved.
ISBN10 #1-56234-450-1 • ISBN13 #978-156234-450-4

Manufactured in the United States
10 9 8 7 6 5 4 3

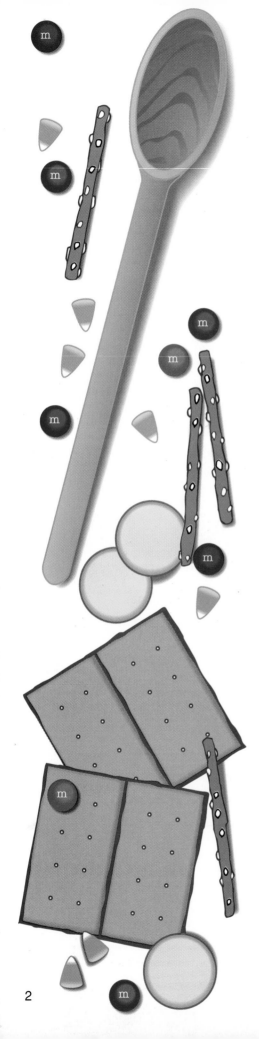

Table of Contents

About This Book

Tie on your apron and don your chef's hat! Cooking with your youngsters will be quick, easy, and satisfying with these recipes designed specifically for young children. Each cooking activity is seasoned with learning opportunities and sprinkled with lots of fun!

Your youngsters will enjoy a helping of the following learning skills and concepts with each hands-on cooking activity:

- Developing oral language and vocabulary
- Emergent reading skills
- Numeral recognition and counting practice
- Multisensory experiences
- Measurement
- Nutrition
- Following step-by-step directions
- Sequencing
- Developing independence

What's the scoop? For each four-page recipe unit, you will find the following:

- A full-color illustration of the finished snack for easy student reference
- A list of ingredients needed to make one serving
- A list of needed utensils and supplies
- A list of timesaving preparation tips
- A full-color perforated page featuring step-by-step recipe cards
- A set of reproducible recipe cards
- A reproducible parent note to request supplies and introduce the snack
- A reproducible student evaluation for each child to complete after the cooking activity
- A related book suggestion for family reading

Remember, many youngsters have allergic reactions to common foods. To ensure a safe and fun snack experience, always consult parents regarding food allergies before students complete these edible projects.

How to Use This Book

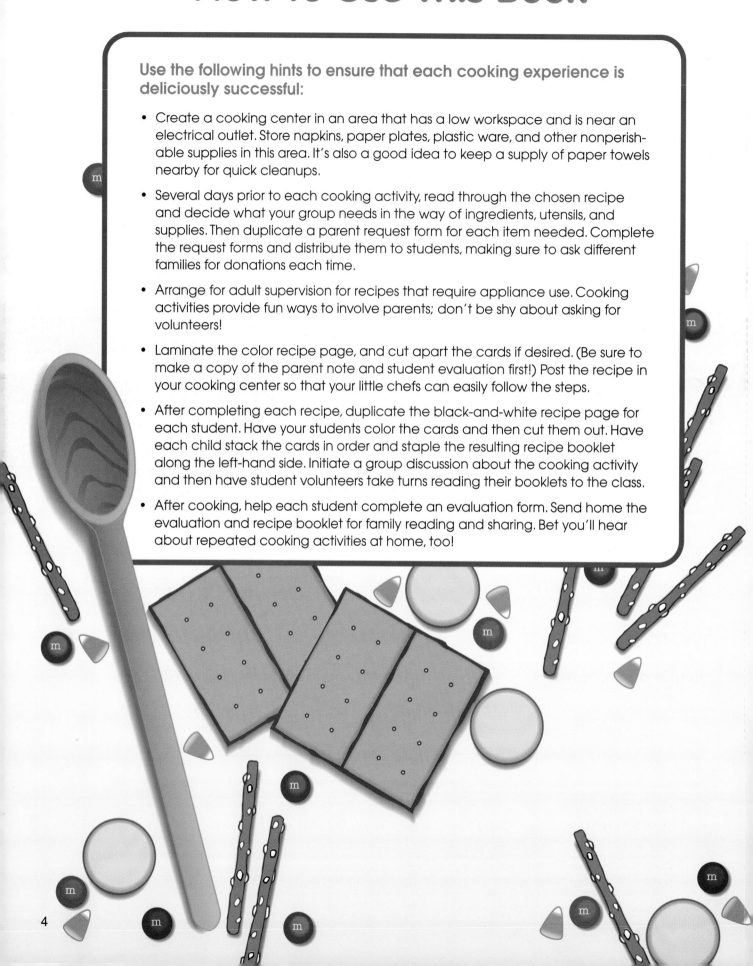

Use the following hints to ensure that each cooking experience is deliciously successful:

- Create a cooking center in an area that has a low workspace and is near an electrical outlet. Store napkins, paper plates, plastic ware, and other nonperishable supplies in this area. It's also a good idea to keep a supply of paper towels nearby for quick cleanups.

- Several days prior to each cooking activity, read through the chosen recipe and decide what your group needs in the way of ingredients, utensils, and supplies. Then duplicate a parent request form for each item needed. Complete the request forms and distribute them to students, making sure to ask different families for donations each time.

- Arrange for adult supervision for recipes that require appliance use. Cooking activities provide fun ways to involve parents; don't be shy about asking for volunteers!

- Laminate the color recipe page, and cut apart the cards if desired. (Be sure to make a copy of the parent note and student evaluation first!) Post the recipe in your cooking center so that your little chefs can easily follow the steps.

- After completing each recipe, duplicate the black-and-white recipe page for each student. Have your students color the cards and then cut them out. Have each child stack the cards in order and staple the resulting recipe booklet along the left-hand side. Initiate a group discussion about the cooking activity and then have student volunteers take turns reading their booklets to the class.

- After cooking, help each student complete an evaluation form. Send home the evaluation and recipe booklet for family reading and sharing. Bet you'll hear about repeated cooking activities at home, too!

School Bus Treat

Beep, beep! Make way for these school bus treats that are sure to make your little chefs "wheely" excited about cooking!

Ingredients for one:
$^1/_2$ of a Hostess® Twinkie® cake (bus)
2 Rolo® candies (wheels)
3 rectangles of a Hershey's®
    milk chocolate bar (windows)
vanilla frosting
1 red Skittles® candy (stop sign)

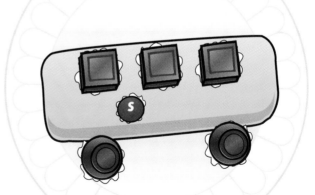

Utensils and supplies:
2 bowls
1 plastic plate
1 small paper plate per child
1 plastic knife per child
napkins

Teacher preparation:
• Cut each Hostess Twinkie cake in half lengthwise. Put each one on the plastic plate.
• Break the chocolate bars into separate rectangles. Place them in a bowl.
• Place the red Skittles candies in a bowl.
• Arrange the ingredients and supplies near the step-by-step direction cards.

School Bus Treat

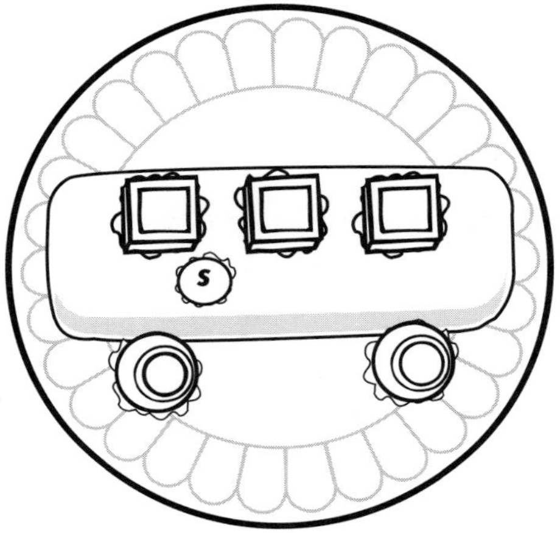

Name ____________________

©2001 The Education Center, Inc. • *Look 'n' Cook* • TEC604

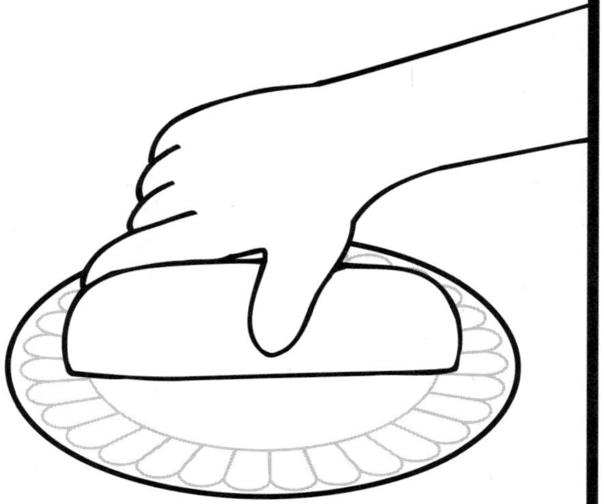

Put 1 cake half on your plate. **1**

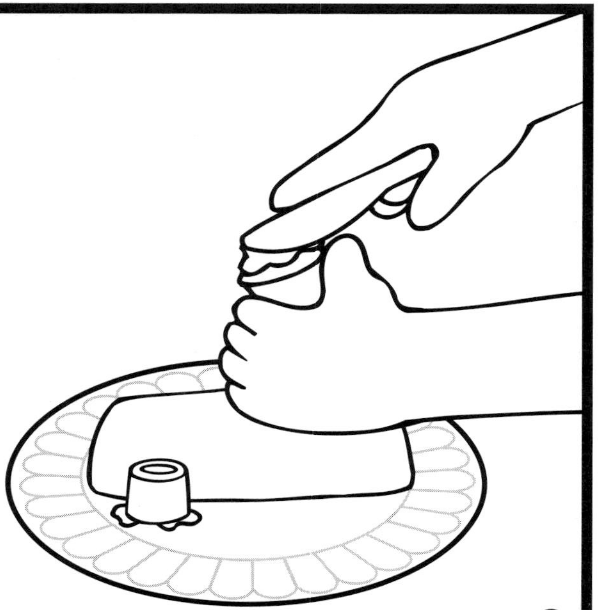

Put on the wheels. **2**

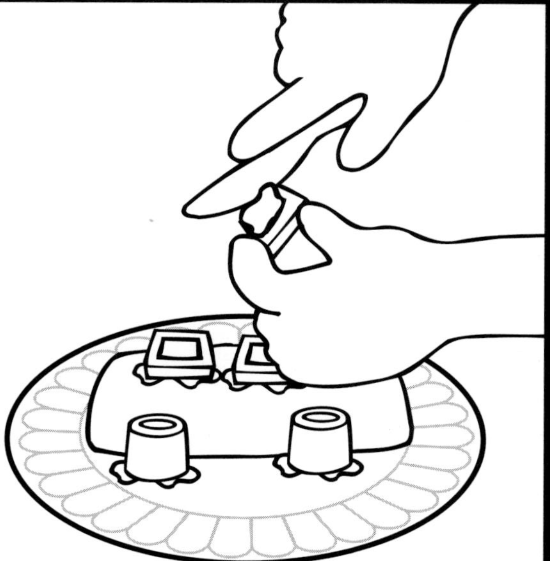

Put on the windows. **3**

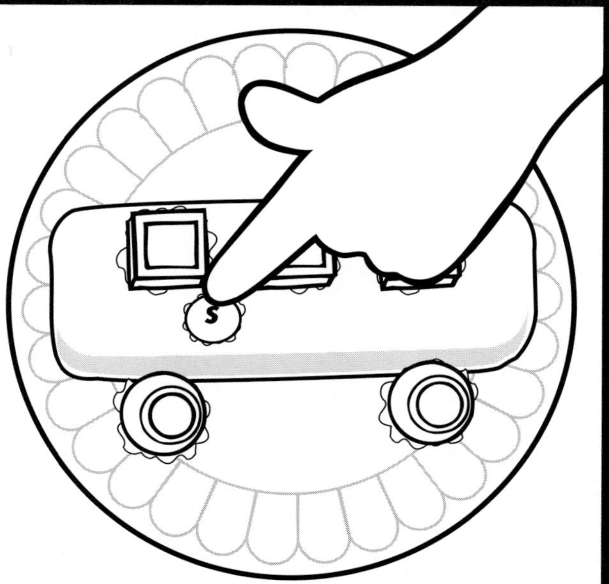

Add a stop sign. **4**

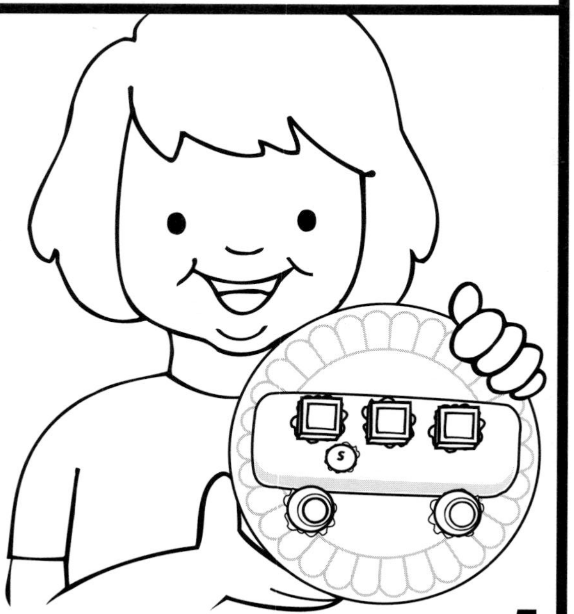

Here comes the bus! **5**

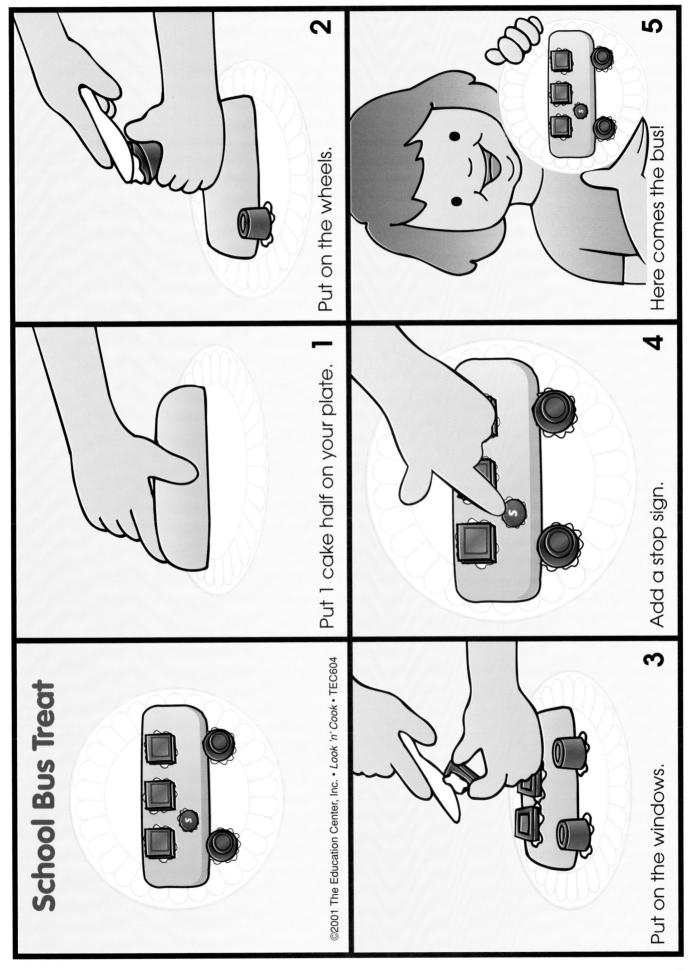

School Bus Treat

2 Put on the wheels.

5 Here comes the bus!

1 Put 1 cake half on your plate.

4 Add a stop sign.

3 Put on the windows.

School Bus Treat

To help celebrate the beginning of school, we're going to follow a simple recipe to make school bus treats. To help us with this cooking project, please send in the item indicated below by _____. Thanks for making your child's learning fun and exciting!

___ box of Hostess® Twinkie® cakes

___ bag of Rolo® candies

___ Hershey's® chocolate bar

___ large bag of Skittles® candies

___ can of vanilla frosting

___ package of napkins

___ package of paper plates

___ package of plastic knives

I made a **School Bus Treat** today!

My favorite part was _____.

It tasted _____.

This is what it looked like:

Chef's signature _____

An extra helping: For more bus fun, look up *The Big Red Bus* by Judy Hindley at your local library. Wheels are wonderful!

Traffic Light

Ready, get set, go! These edible traffic lights will rev up your hungry youngsters in record time!

Ingredients for one:
1 graham cracker sheet
creamy peanut butter
1 unpeeled green apple slice (green light)
1 unpeeled yellow apple slice (yellow light)
1 unpeeled red apple slice (red light)

Utensils and supplies:
3 bowls
1 plastic knife per child
napkins

Teacher preparation:
- Wash the apples; then slice them.
- Separate apple slices by color; then put each color in a different bowl.
- If desired, toss the sliced apples with diluted lemon juice or lemon-lime soda to prevent browning.
- Arrange the ingredients and supplies near the step-by-step direction cards.

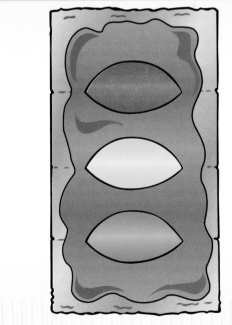

Traffic Light

Name _____

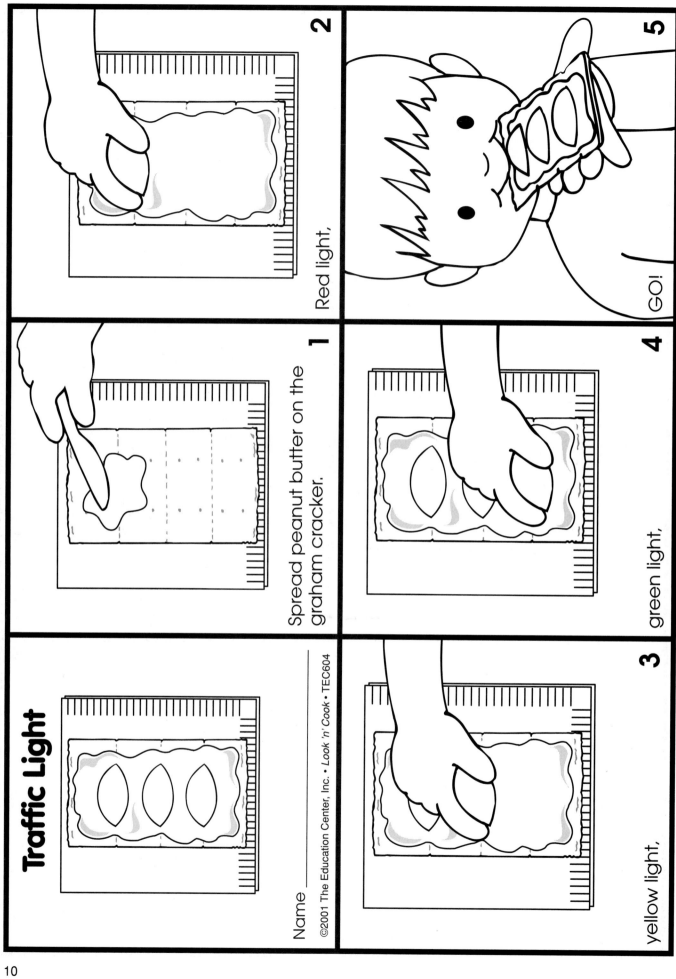

1 Spread peanut butter on the graham cracker.

2 Red light,

3 yellow light,

4 green light,

5 GO!

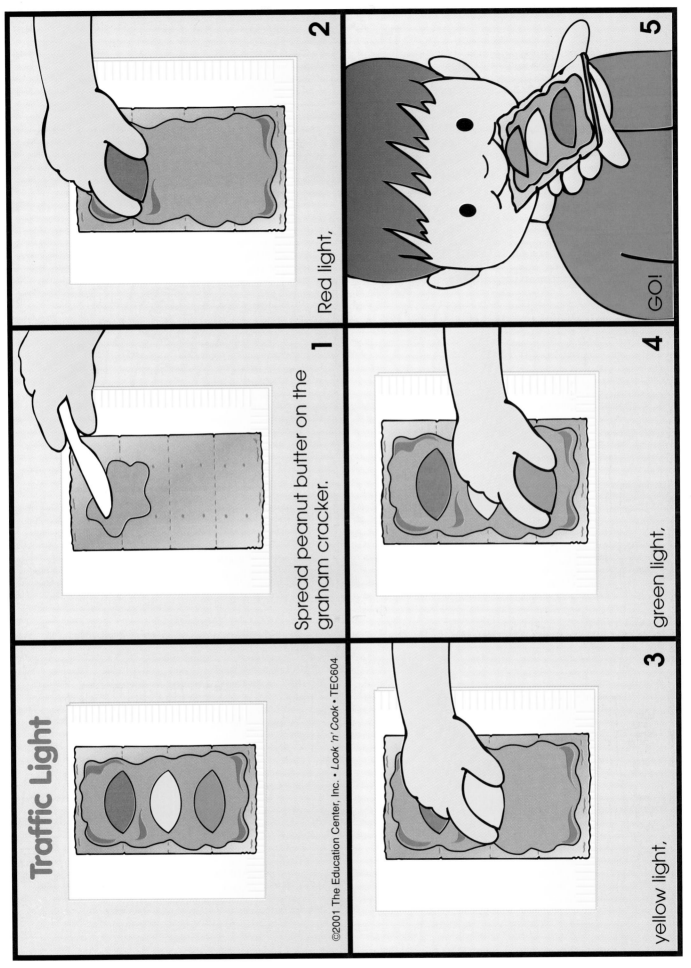

Traffic Light

2

1

Spread peanut butter on the graham cracker.

3

yellow light,

4

green light,

5

Red light,

GO!

©2001 The Education Center, Inc. • *Look 'n' Cook* • TEC604

Traffic Light

There's no better way of learning about traffic lights and road safety than by following directions to make a miniature traffic light! To help us with this cooking project, please send in the item indicated below by _____. Thanks for making your child's learning fun and exciting!

___ bag of red apples

___ bag of green apples

___ bag of yellow apples

___ jar of creamy peanut butter

___ box of graham crackers

___ package of napkins

___ package of plastic knives

I made a **Traffic Light** in school today!

My favorite part was _____.

It tasted _____.

This is what it looked like:

Chef's signature _____

An extra helping: For more information about traffic lights and road signs, read *Red, Yellow, Green...What Do Signs Mean?* by Joan Holub.

Awesome Apple Tree

Your little ones are sure to fall for these tasty apple tree treats! Make them to welcome autumn or to celebrate Johnny Appleseed's birthday on September 26.

Ingredients for one:
1 round butter cracker
vanilla frosting
1 pretzel stick (tree trunk)
5 red, green, or yellow
    M&M's® candies (apples)

Utensils and supplies:
1 plastic knife per child
3 bowls
green food coloring
napkins

Teacher preparation:
- Tint the frosting with green food coloring.
- Sort the red, green, and yellow M&M's into separate bowls.
- Arrange the ingredients and supplies near the step-by-step direction cards.

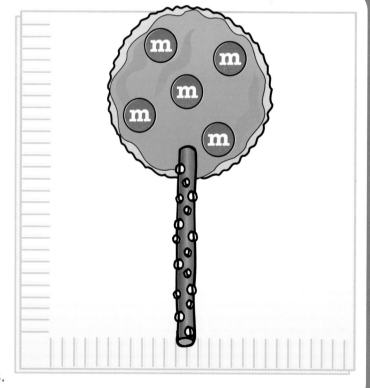

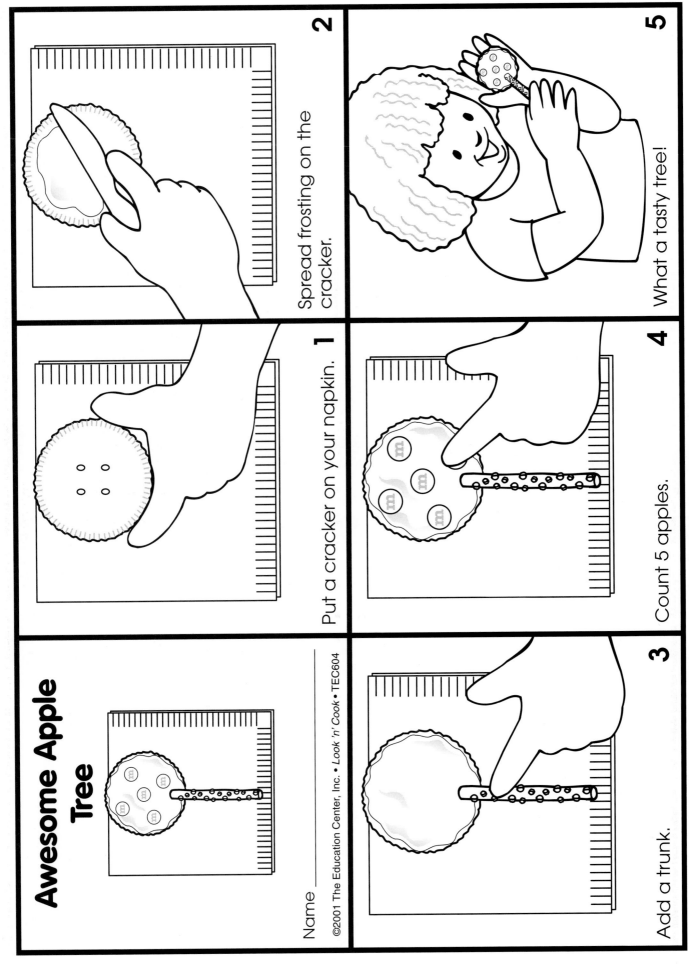

2

Spread frosting on the cracker.

5

What a tasty tree!

1

Put a cracker on your napkin.

4

Count 5 apples.

Awesome Apple Tree

Name _____

©2001 The Education Center, Inc. • Look 'n' Cook • TEC604

3

Add a trunk.

Awesome Apple Tree

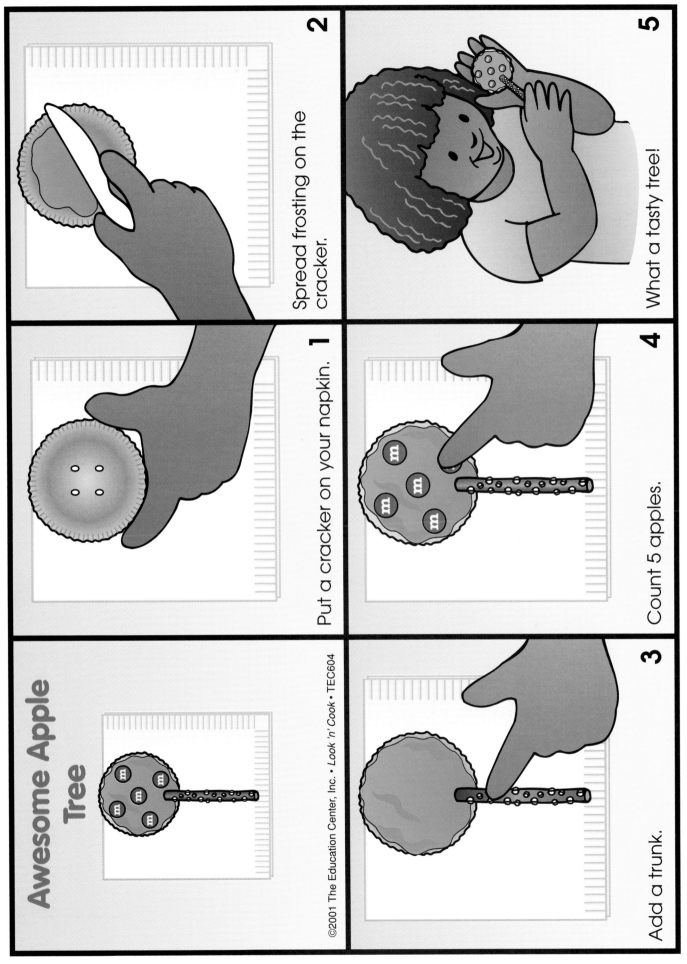

2 Spread frosting on the cracker.

5 What a tasty tree!

1 Put a cracker on your napkin.

4 Count 5 apples.

3 Add a trunk.

Awesome Apple Tree

Autumn is upon us! In school, we are going to make apple trees to munch and crunch. To help us with this cooking project, please send in the item indicated below by _____. Thanks for making your child's learning fun and exciting!

___ box of round butter crackers

___ can of vanilla frosting

___ package of food coloring

___ bag of small pretzel sticks

___ large bag of M&M's® candies

___ package of napkins

___ package of plastic knives

I made an **Awesome Apple Tree** in school today!

My favorite part was _____.

It tasted _____.

This is what it looked like:

Chef's signature _____

An extra helping: Check out *Johnny Appleseed Goes A'planting* by Patsy Jensen at your local library for some interesting apple facts!

Cinnamon Puffs

These sweet treats will make any day of the year special! While enjoying the snack, have your youngsters brainstorm other spherical items. Everyone is sure to have a ball!

Ingredients for one:
1 piece of refrigerated biscuit dough
squeeze margarine
cinnamon sugar (in a shaker)

Utensils and supplies:
1 plastic knife per child
1 foil cupcake liner per child
permanent marker
baking sheet
oven
napkins

Teacher preparation:
• Use a permanent marker to personalize the outside bottom of a foil cupcake liner for each child.
• Arrange the ingredients and supplies near the step-by-step direction cards.
• Place the cinnamon puffs on a baking sheet and bake them according to the package directions.

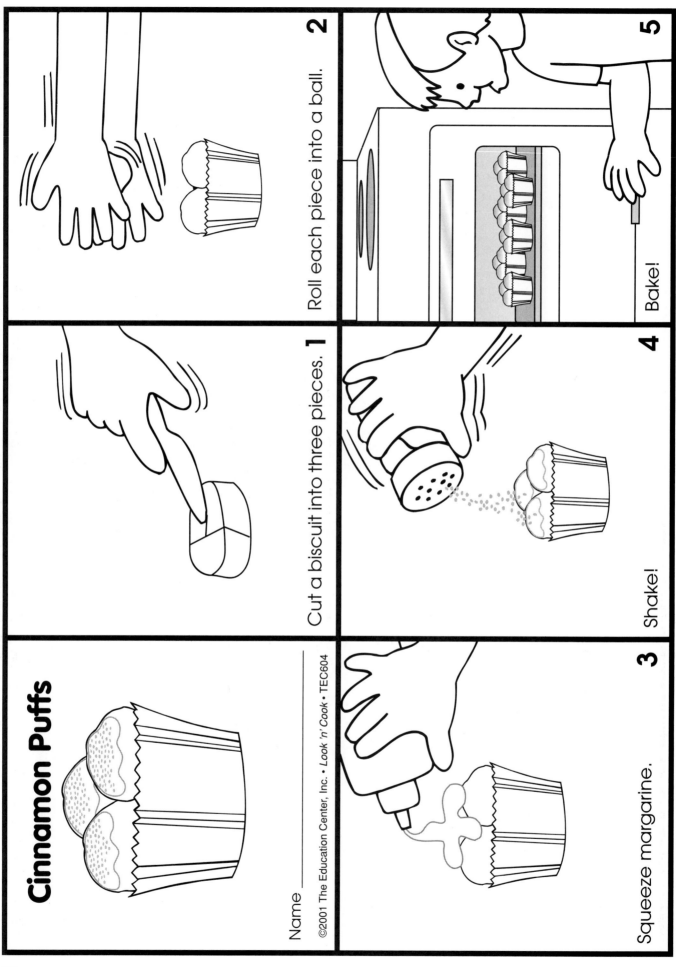

Cinnamon Puffs

Name _____

©2001 The Education Center, Inc. • Look 'n' Cook • TEC604

1 Cut a biscuit into three pieces.

2 Roll each piece into a ball.

3 Squeeze margarine.

4 Shake!

5 Bake!

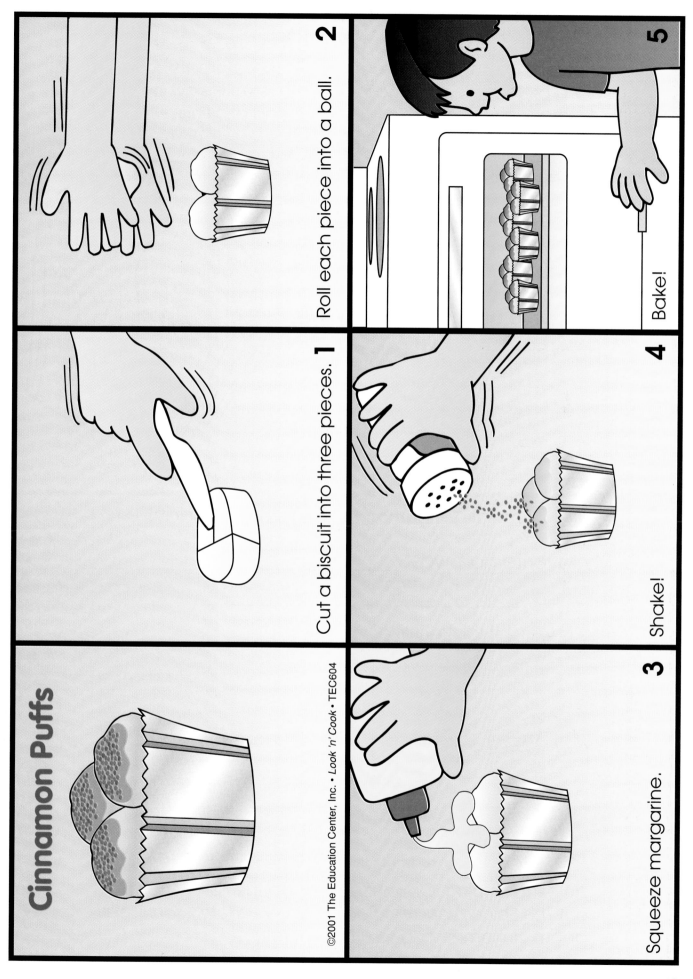

Cinnamon Puffs

2 Roll each piece into a ball.

5 Bake!

1 Cut a biscuit into three pieces.

4 Shake!

3 Squeeze margarine.

©2001 The Education Center, Inc. • *Look 'n' Cook* • TEC604

Cinnamon Puffs

Our class will be busy baking some sweet-to-eat treats! To help us with this cooking project, please send in the item listed below by _____. Thanks for making your child's learning fun and exciting!

___ can of refrigerated biscuits

___ cinnamon sugar

___ squeezable margarine

___ package of foil cupcake liners

___ package of napkins

___ package of plastic knives

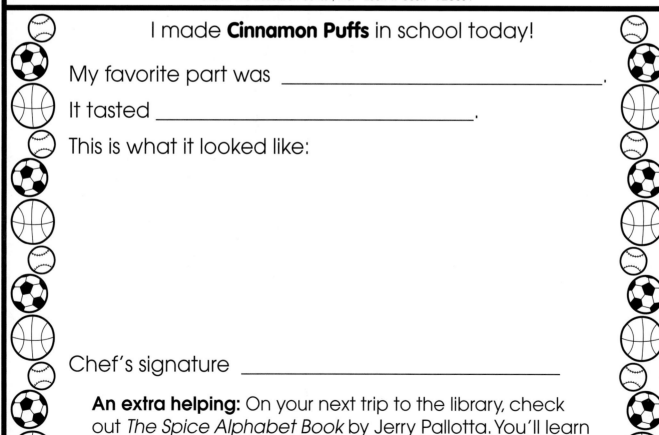

I made **Cinnamon Puffs** in school today!

My favorite part was _____.

It tasted _____.

This is what it looked like:

Chef's signature _____

An extra helping: On your next trip to the library, check out *The Spice Alphabet Book* by Jerry Pallotta. You'll learn about cinnamon and so much more!

Apple Slaw Sandwich

Get to the core of cooking with this "grate" snack idea!

Ingredients for one:
2 tbsp. grated apple (approximately $1/2$ of a small apple)
1 tsp. honey
1 tsp. peanut butter
10 raisins
1 slice of bread

Utensils and supplies:
1 knife
food grater
1 bowl
1 tablespoon
1 teaspoon
1 8-oz. plastic cup per child
1 plastic spoon per child
napkins

Teacher preparation:
- Peel, core, and then grate a class supply of apples. Place the grated apple in the bowl.
- If desired, toss the grated apples with diluted lemon juice or lemon-lime soda to prevent browning.
- Arrange the ingredients and supplies near the step-by-step direction cards.

Apple Slaw Sandwich

2 Add 1 teaspoon of honey.

5 Make an apple slaw sandwich!

1 Put 2 tablespoons of grated apple in a cup.

4 Count 10 raisins. Stir your slaw.

Name _____

©2001 The Education Center, Inc. • Look 'n' Cook • TEC604

3 Add 1 teaspoon of peanut butter.

2 Add 1 teaspoon of honey.

5 Make an apple slaw sandwich!

1 Put 2 tablespoons of grated apple in a cup.

4 Count 10 raisins. Stir your slaw.

3 Add 1 teaspoon of peanut butter.

Apple Slaw Sandwich

©2001 The Education Center, Inc. • *Look 'n' Cook* • TEC604

23

Apple Slaw Sandwich

We're going to stir up some fun in our classroom with a unique apple recipe! To help us with this cooking project, please send in the item indicated below by _____. Thanks for making your child's learning fun and exciting!

___ bag of apples

___ jar of peanut butter

___ jar of honey

___ large box of raisins

___ loaf of sandwich bread

___ package of plastic spoons

___ package of 8-oz. plastic cups

___ package of napkins

I made an **Apple Slaw Sandwich** in school today!

My favorite part was _____.

It tasted _____.

This is what it looked like:

Chef's signature _____

An extra helping: On your next visit to the library, pick *The Seasons of Arnold's Apple Tree* by Gail Gibbons. Read all about those tasty red apples!

Camera Cookie

One, two, three...SMILE! After taking some photos of your youngsters, have them make these camera cookies that will be gone in a snap!

Ingredients for one:
1 graham cracker sheet
creamy peanut butter
1 vanilla wafer
1 red M&M's® candy (light)
1 green M&M's candy (shutter release)
1 yellow M&M's candy (flash)
1 brown M&M's candy (lens)
1 8" length of licorice lace (handle)

Utensils and supplies:
4 plastic bowls
1 plastic knife per child
napkins

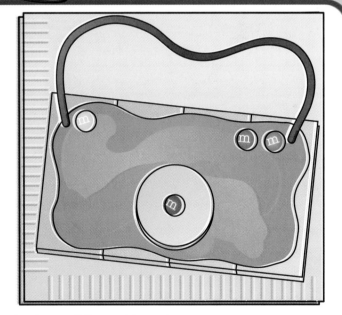

Teacher preparation:
- Sort the M&M's candies and put each color in a different bowl.
- Cut an eight-inch length of licorice lace for each child.
- Arrange the ingredients and supplies near the step-by-step direction cards.

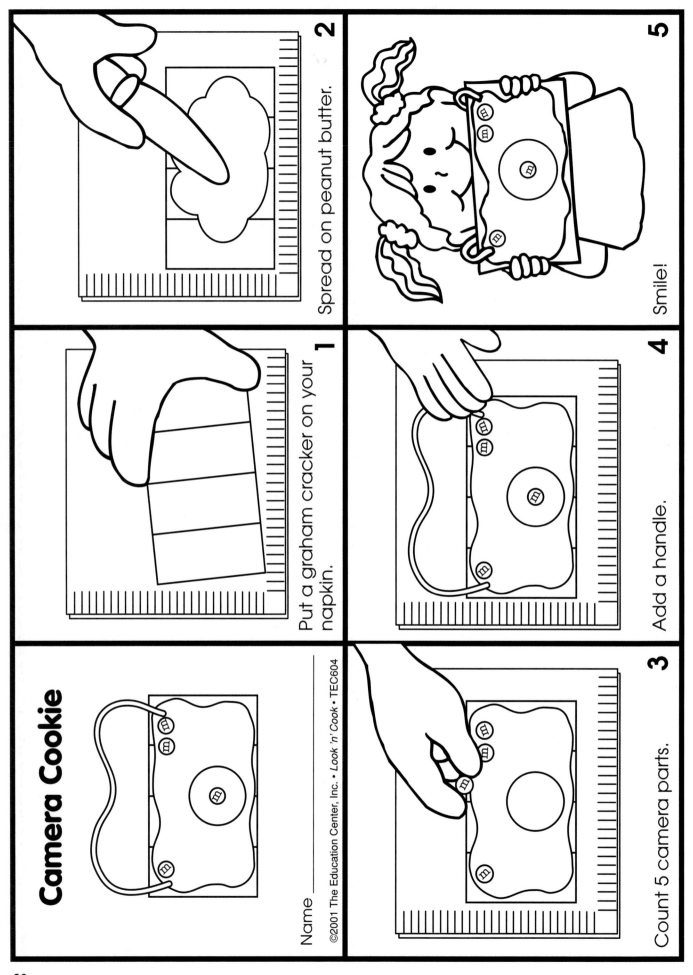

Camera Cookie

Name _____

©2001 The Education Center, Inc. • *Look 'n' Cook* • TEC604

1 Put a graham cracker on your napkin.

2 Spread on peanut butter.

3 Count 5 camera parts.

4 Add a handle.

5 Smile!

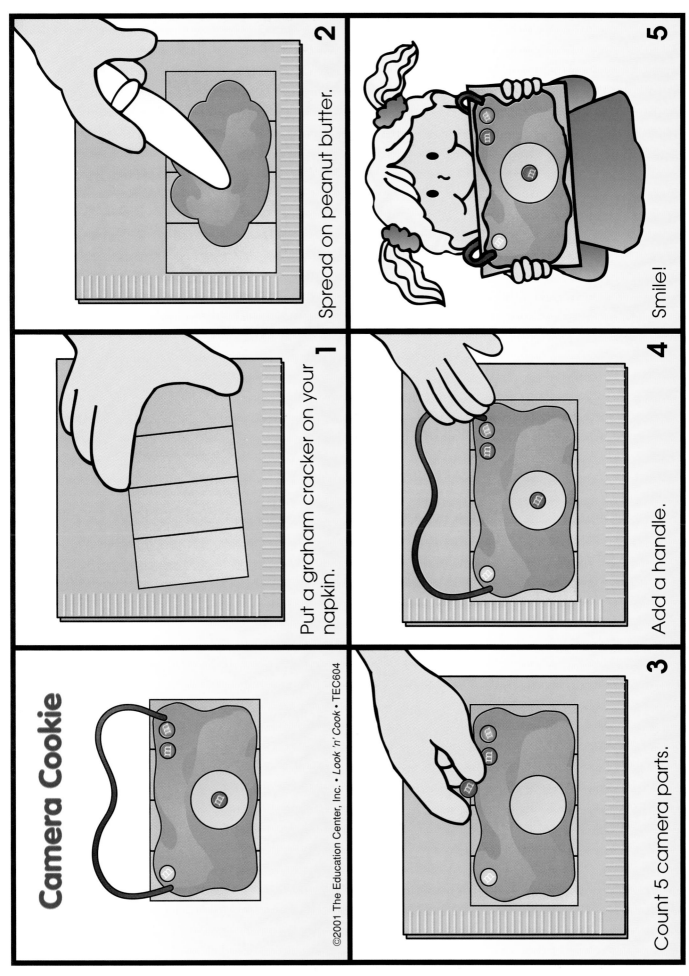

Camera Cookie

1 Put a graham cracker on your napkin.

2 Spread on peanut butter.

3 Count 5 camera parts.

4 Add a handle.

5 Smile!

©2001 The Education Center, Inc. • *Look 'n' Cook* • TEC604

Camera Cookie

Everyone knows that cameras create precious memories as well as smiles. To celebrate our classroom photo shoot, we will be making Camera Cookies to munch on. To help us with this cooking project, please send in the item indicated below by _____. Thanks for making your child's learning fun and exciting!

___ box of graham crackers

___ box of vanilla wafers

___ jar of creamy peanut butter

___ package of black licorice laces

___ large bag of M&M's® candies

___ package of napkins

___ package of plastic knives

Smile! I made a **Camera Cookie** in school today!

My favorite part was _____.

It tasted _____.

This is what it looked like:

Chef's signature _____

An extra helping: For more camera fun, check out *Alfred's Camera* by David Ellwand at your local library. You won't be able to stop smiling!

Cool Jack-o'-Lantern

It's pumpkin time! Have your youngsters make this creamy, cool snack, and then have them share stories about carving real jack-o'-lanterns.

Ingredients for one:
1 scoop of orange sherbet (pumpkin)
8 pieces of candy corn (jack-o'-lantern
   face)
1 green gumdrop (stem)

Utensils and supplies:
ice-cream scoop
1 disposable bowl per child
1 plastic spoon per child
napkins

Teacher preparation:
- Allow sherbet to soften slightly.
- Arrange the ingredients and supplies
  near the step-by-step direction cards.

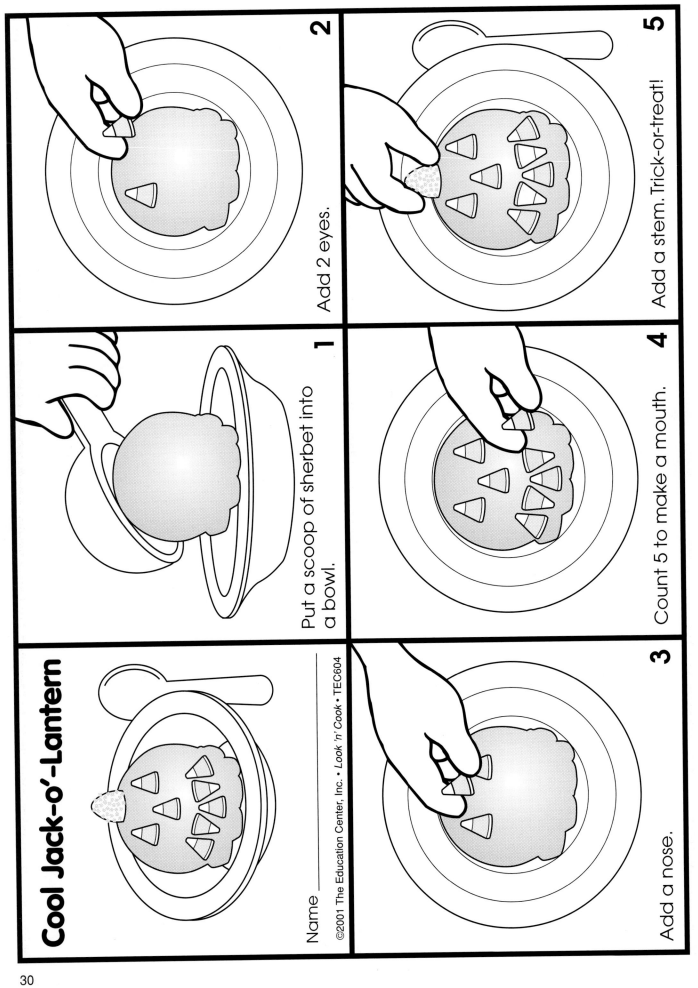

Cool Jack-o'-Lantern

Name _____

2 Add 2 eyes.

5 Add a stem. Trick-or-treat!

1 Put a scoop of sherbet into a bowl.

4 Count 5 to make a mouth.

3 Add a nose.

©2001 The Education Center, Inc. • Look 'n' Cook • TEC604

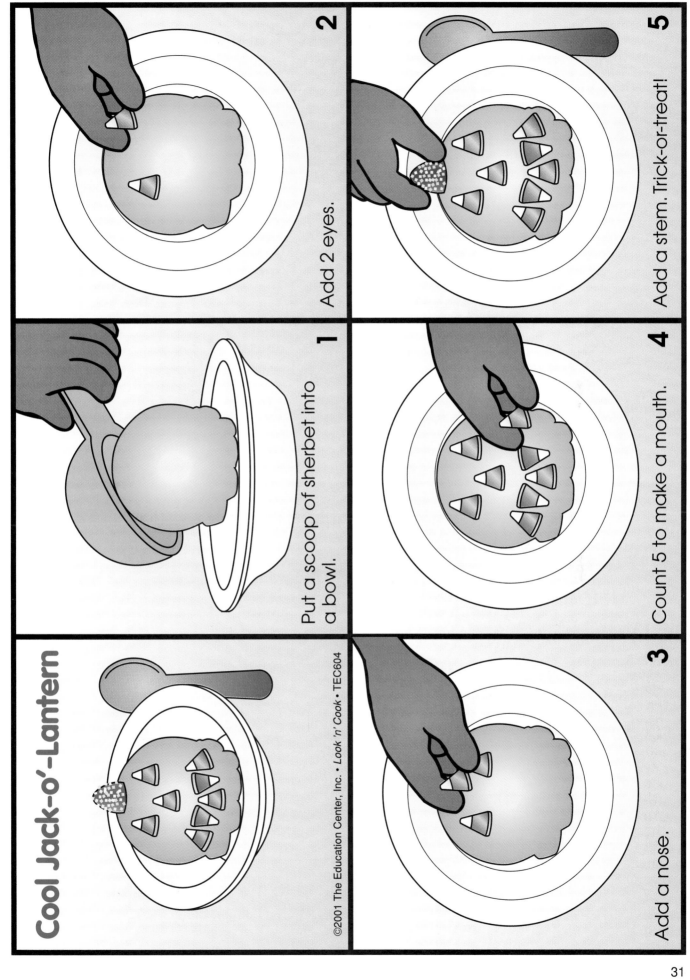

Cool Jack-o'-Lantern

1 Put a scoop of sherbet into a bowl.

2 Add 2 eyes.

3 Add a nose.

4 Count 5 to make a mouth.

5 Add a stem. Trick-or-treat!

©2001 The Education Center, Inc. • Look 'n' Cook • TEC604

31

Cool Jack-o'-Lantern

Raking leaves, picking pumpkins, carving jack-o'-lanterns…These are some of the pastimes we enjoy during October. In school, we're going to create miniature jack-o'-lanterns for a cool snack! To help us with this cooking project, please send in the item indicated below by _____. Thanks for making your child's learning fun and exciting!

___ container of orange sherbet

___ bag of green gumdrops

___ bag of candy corn

___ package of disposable bowls

___ package of plastic spoons

___ package of napkins

I made a **Cool Jack-o'-Lantern** in school today!

My favorite part was _____.

It tasted _____.

This is what it looked like:

Chef's signature _____

An extra helping: On your next trip to the library, look for *The Perky Little Pumpkin* by Margaret Friskey. Boo!

Candy Corn Wreath

There's corn aplenty in autumn, so while your students are learning about harvesttime, have them make miniature corn wreaths— with colorful candy corn!

Ingredients for one:
1 ring-shaped butter cookie
vanilla frosting
5 pieces of candy corn
5 pieces of Indian candy corn

Utensils and supplies:
1 plastic knife per child
napkins

Teacher preparation:
• Arrange the ingredients and supplies near the step-by-step direction cards.

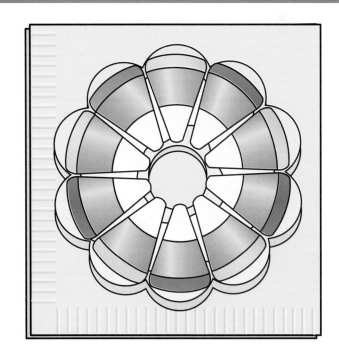

Candy Corn Wreath

Name _____

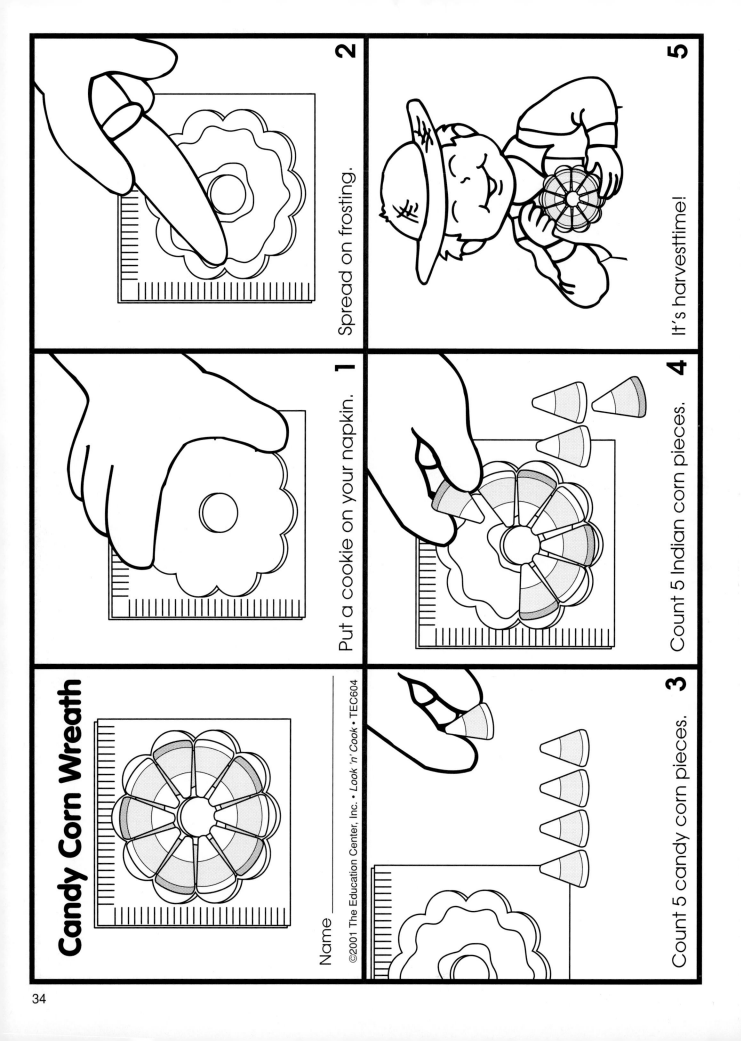

1 Put a cookie on your napkin.

2 Spread on frosting.

3 Count 5 candy corn pieces.

4 Count 5 Indian corn pieces.

5 It's harvesttime!

Candy Corn Wreath

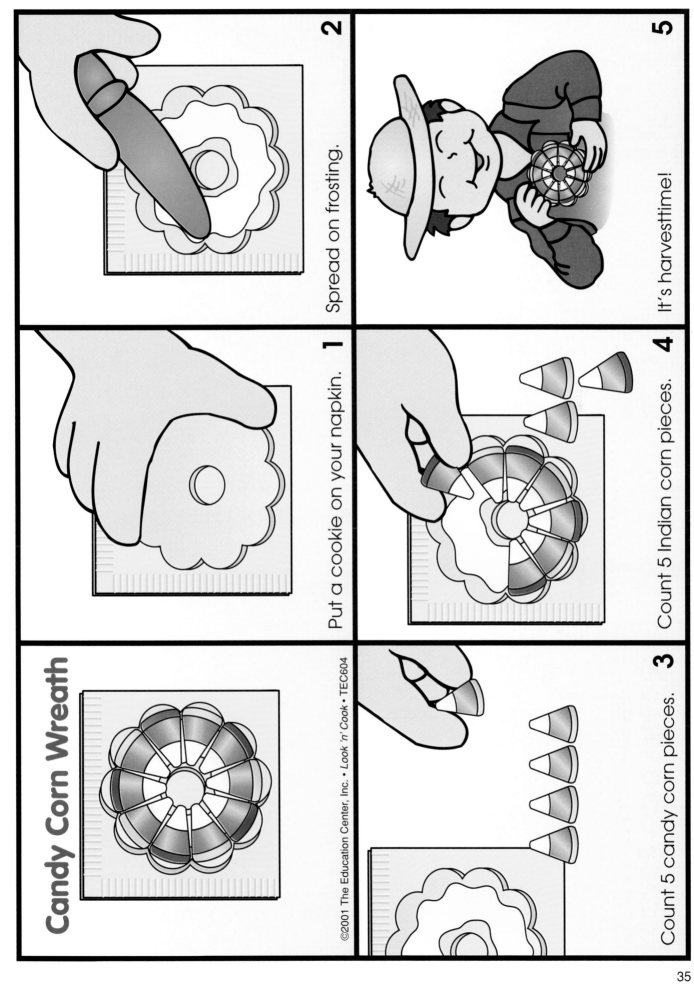

1 Put a cookie on your napkin.

2 Spread on frosting.

3 Count 5 candy corn pieces.

4 Count 5 Indian corn pieces.

5 It's harvesttime!

©2001 The Education Center, Inc. • *Look 'n' Cook* • TEC604

Candy Corn Wreath

School is full of treats, especially at this time of year! Your child will be making a miniature candy corn wreath to celebrate harvesttime. To help us with this cooking project, please send in the item indicated below by _____. Thanks for making your child's learning fun and exciting!

___ package of ring-shaped
     butter cookies

___ can of vanilla frosting

___ bag of candy corn

___ bag of Indian candy corn

___ package of napkins

___ package of plastic knives

I made a **Candy Corn Wreath** in school today!

My favorite part was _____.

It tasted _____.

This is what it looked like:

Chef's signature _____

An extra helping: Check out *Raccoons and Ripe Corn* by Jim Arnosky at your local library. What an autumn treat!

Creepy Claws

These handy treats will satisfy even your hungriest critters!

Ingredients for one:
sugar cookie dough
vanilla frosting
5 pieces of candy corn (claws)
5 M&M's® candies (warts)
1 spice drop (ring)

Utensils and supplies:
green food coloring
rolling pin
hand-shaped cookie cutter
toaster oven
4" square of aluminum foil per child
baking sheet
1 plastic knife per child
napkins
permanent marker

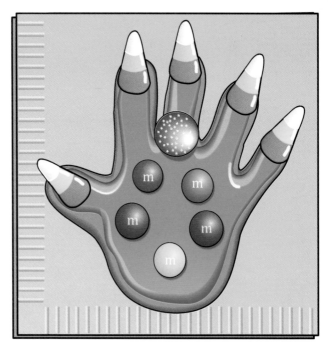

Teacher preparation:
• Personalize a foil square for each child.
• Tint the frosting with green food coloring.
• Cut a small portion of dough for each child.
• Arrange the ingredients and supplies near the step-by-step direction cards.
• Bake cookies according to package directions.

Creepy Claws

Name _____

©2001 The Education Center, Inc. • *Look 'n' Cook* • TEC604

1 Roll out the dough.

2 Cut out a hand shape. Bake.

3 Spread frosting on the hand.

4 Count 5 creepy claws. Count 5 warts.

5 Add a ring. Oooh—creepy!

Creepy Claws

1 Roll out the dough.

2 Cut out a hand shape. Bake.

3 Spread frosting on the hand.

4 Count 5 creepy claws. Count 5 warts.

5 Add a ring. Oooh—creepy!

Ella

Creepy Claws

Our classroom will be "paws-atively" full of fun when we make a batch of cute monster paws to munch! To help us with this cooking project, please send in the item indicated below by _____. Thanks for making your child's learning fun and exciting!

___ roll of refrigerated sugar cookie dough

___ can of vanilla frosting

___ large bag of candy corn

___ large bag of M&M's® candies

___ large bag of spice drops

___ package of food coloring

___ package of plastic knives

___ roll of aluminum foil

___ package of napkins

I made **Creepy Claws** in school today.

My favorite part was _____.

It tasted _____.

This is what it looked like:

Chef's signature _____

An extra helping: Don't forget to grab a monster book at the library! Look for *One Hungry Monster: A Counting Book in Rhyme* by Susan Heyboer O'Keefe.

Wobble Gobble

These colorful turkey cookies will be gobbled up in no time!

Ingredients for one:
1 fudge-striped cookie
1 Nutter Butter® cookie
1 candy corn
2 chocolate chips
red tube frosting

Utensils and supplies:
napkins

Teacher preparation:
• Arrange the ingredients and supplies near the step-by-step direction cards.

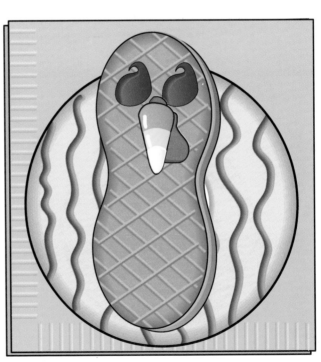

Wobble Gobble

2 Put a peanut cookie on top.

5 Gobble, gobble, gone!

1 Put a round cookie on your napkin.

Name _____

©2001 The Education Center, Inc. • *Look 'n' Cook* • TEC604

4 Add a beak. Add a wattle.

3 Count two eyes.

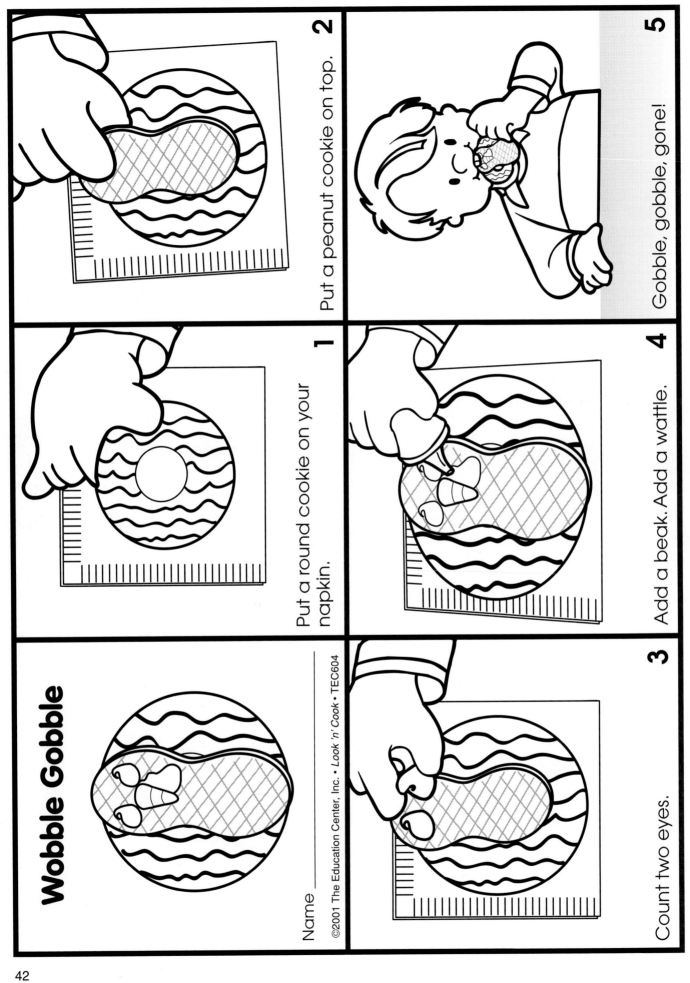

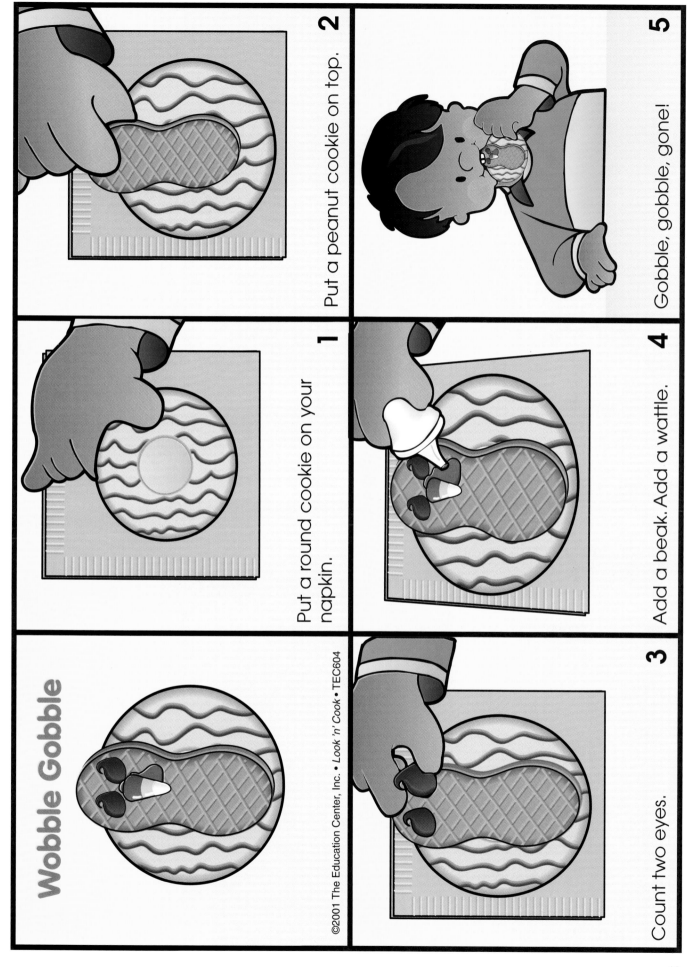

Wobble Gobble

2 Put a peanut cookie on top.

5 Gobble, gobble, gone!

1 Put a round cookie on your napkin.

4 Add a beak. Add a wattle.

3 Count two eyes.

©2001 The Education Center, Inc. • *Look 'n' Cook* • TEC604

43

Wobble Gobble

Thanksgiving is right around the corner! Our class is thankful for many things and snacktime is one of them! To help us with this cooking project, please send in the item indicated below by _____. Thanks for making your child's learning fun and exciting!

___ package of fudge-striped cookies

___ package of Nutter Butter® cookies

___ large bag of candy corn

___ bag of milk chocolate chips

___ small tube of red frosting

___ package of napkins

I made a **Wobble Gobble** in school today!

My favorite part was _____.

It tasted _____.

This is what it looked like:

Chef's signature _____

An extra helping: Check out *'Twas the Night Before Thanksgiving* by Dav Pilkey on your next trip to the library! What a silly book!

North Pole Peppermint Float

Ahhh, peppermint! 'Tis the season for festive treats, so have your little chefs make these oh-so-refreshing drinks.

Ingredients for one:
1 scoop of vanilla ice cream
$1/2$ c. ginger ale
miniature candy cane
red and green sugar crystals

Utensils and supplies:
ice-cream scoop
one 8-oz. clear plastic cup per child
measuring cup
1 straw per child
napkins

Teacher preparation:
• Unwrap the candy canes.
• Allow ice cream to soften slightly.
• Arrange the ingredients and supplies near the step-by-step direction cards.

North Pole Peppermint Float

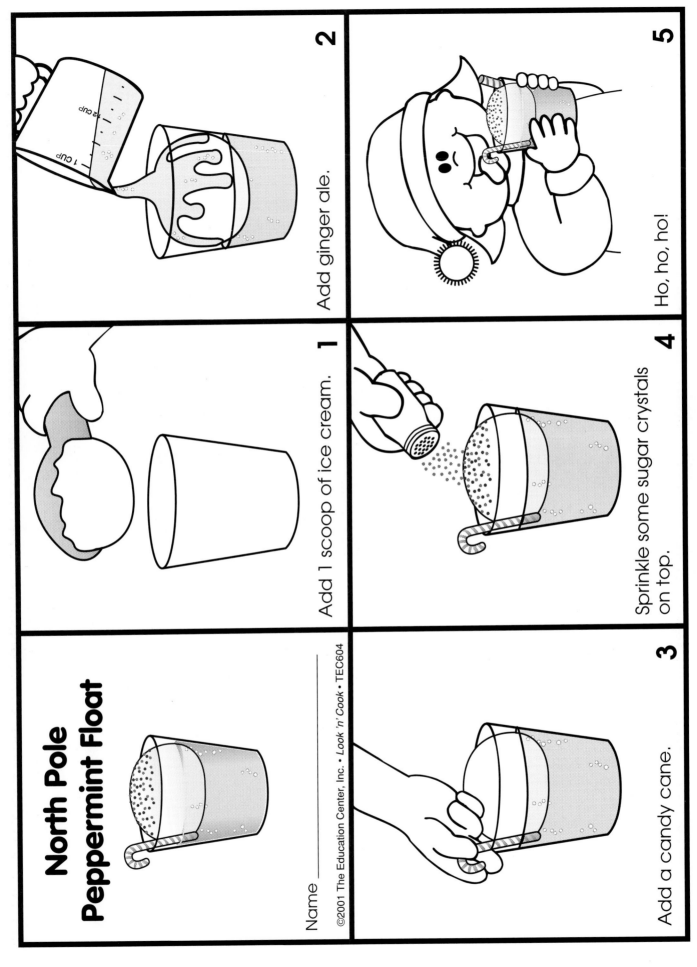

2 Add ginger ale.

5 Ho, ho, ho!

1 Add 1 scoop of ice cream.

4 Sprinkle some sugar crystals on top.

3 Add a candy cane.

Name _____

North Pole Peppermint Float

1 Add 1 scoop of ice cream.

2 Add ginger ale.

3 Add a candy cane.

4 Sprinkle some sugar crystals on top.

5 Ho, ho, ho!

©2001 The Education Center, Inc. • Look 'n' Cook • TEC604

47

North Pole Peppermint Float

We are going to follow a simple recipe to make a festive and wintry treat. To help us with this cooking project, please send in the item checked below by _____. Thanks for making your child's learning fun and exciting!

___ miniature candy canes

___ container of vanilla ice cream

___ liter of ginger ale

___ container of red sugar crystals

___ container of green sugar crystals

___ package of 8-oz. clear plastic cups

___ package of straws

___ package of napkins

I made a **North Pole Peppermint Float** in school today!

My favorite part was _____.

It tasted _____.

This is what it looked like:

Chef's signature _____

An extra helping: Look for *The Candystore Man* by Jonathan London at your local library. There's nothing sweeter!

Evergreen Delight

Looking "fir" a recipe to go along with an evergreen or Christmas theme? This snack is simple and delicious and will quickly disappear!

Ingredients for 4–6 trees:
6 c. crispy rice cereal
1 package of marshmallows
3 tbsp. margarine
vegetable cooking spray
Skittles® candies

Utensils and supplies:
microwave oven
large microwave-safe bowl
waxed paper
mixing spoon
green food coloring
napkins
scissors

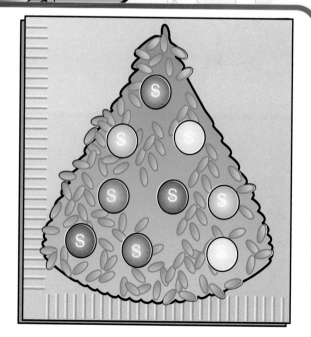

Teacher preparation:
- Cut a six-inch square of waxed paper for each child.
- Follow the microwave directions on a box of crispy rice cereal for making crispy rice treats. Tint the mixture with green food coloring and allow it to cool—but not harden—before having children mold it.
- Arrange the ingredients and supplies near the step-by-step direction cards.

Evergreen Delight

Name _____

©2001 The Education Center, Inc. • *Look 'n' Cook* • TEC604

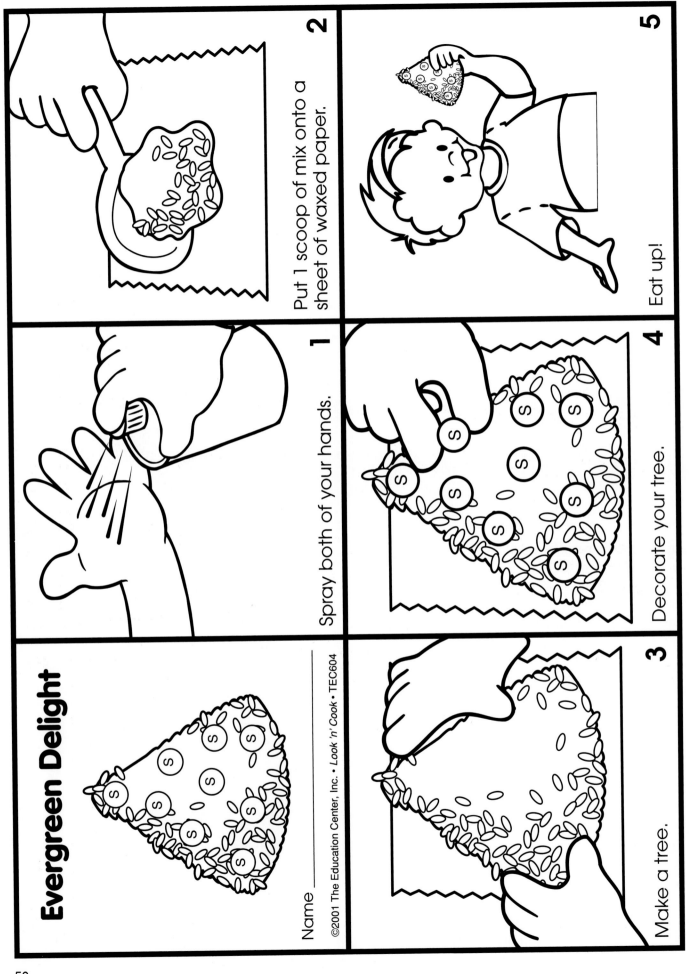

1 Spray both of your hands.

2 Put 1 scoop of mix onto a sheet of waxed paper.

3 Make a tree.

4 Decorate your tree.

5 Eat up!

50

Evergreen Delight

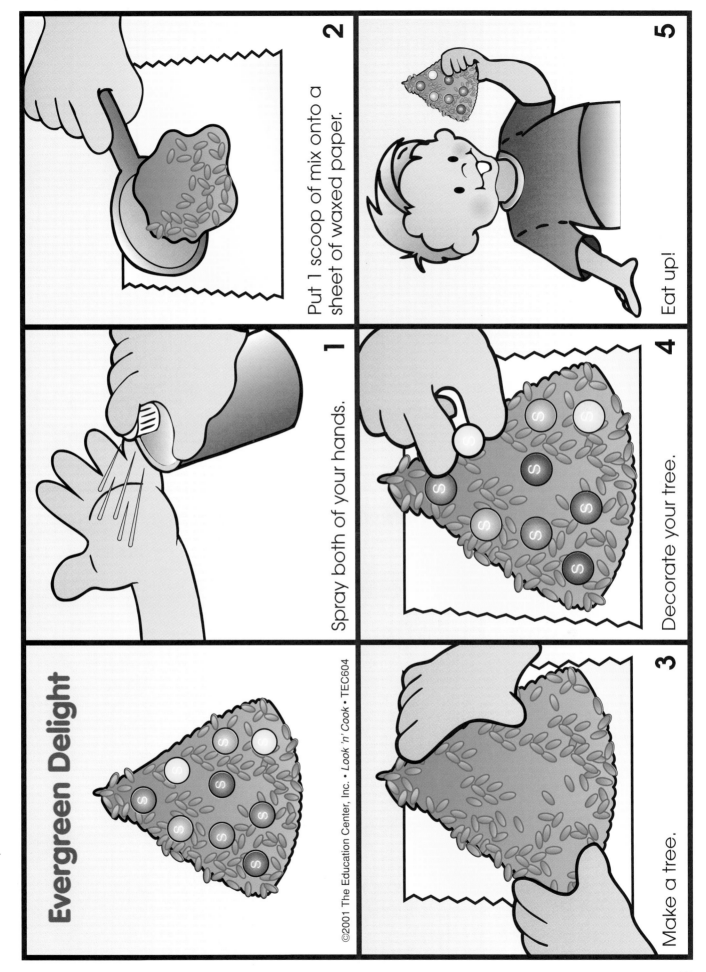

2

Put 1 scoop of mix onto a sheet of waxed paper.

5

Eat up!

1

Spray both of your hands.

©2001 The Education Center, Inc. • *Look 'n' Cook* • TEC604

4

Decorate your tree.

3

Make a tree.

Evergreen Delight

To celebrate the winter season, we're going to make some "tree-licious" snacks! To help us with this cooking project, please send in the item indicated below by _____. Thanks for making your child's learning fun and exciting!

___ box of crispy rice cereal

___ bag of white marshmallows

___ tub of margarine

___ roll of waxed paper

___ large bag of Skittles® candies

___ vegetable cooking spray

___ package of food coloring

___ package of napkins

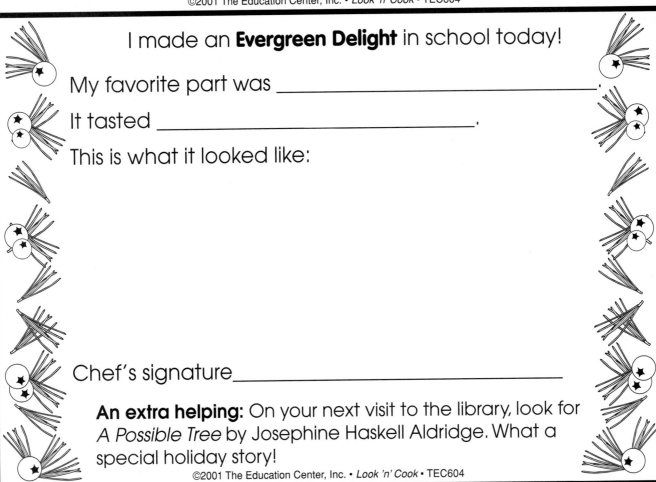

I made an **Evergreen Delight** in school today!

My favorite part was _____.

It tasted _____.

This is what it looked like:

Chef's signature_____

An extra helping: On your next visit to the library, look for *A Possible Tree* by Josephine Haskell Aldridge. What a special holiday story!

Silly Snow Pal Snack

Whether there is snow on the ground or not, your youngsters will have heaps of fun making these silly snow pals!

Ingredients for one:
1 scoop of vanilla frozen yogurt
2 chocolate chips
1 maraschino cherry
3 M&M's® Minis® baking bits
1 Hershey's® Kisses® candy

Utensils and supplies:
ice-cream scoop
1 disposable bowl per child
1 plastic spoon per child
napkins

Teacher preparation:
• Allow frozen yogurt to soften slightly.
• Arrange the ingredients and supplies near the step-by-step direction cards.

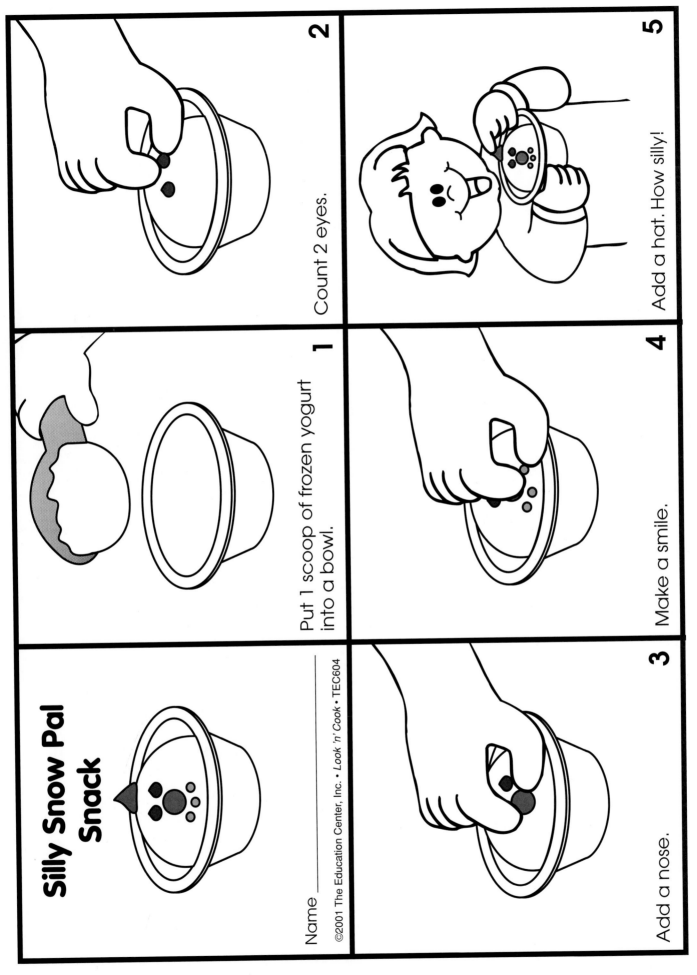

2

Count 2 eyes.

5

Add a hat. How silly!

1

Put 1 scoop of frozen yogurt into a bowl.

4

Make a smile.

Silly Snow Pal Snack

Name _____

3

Add a nose.

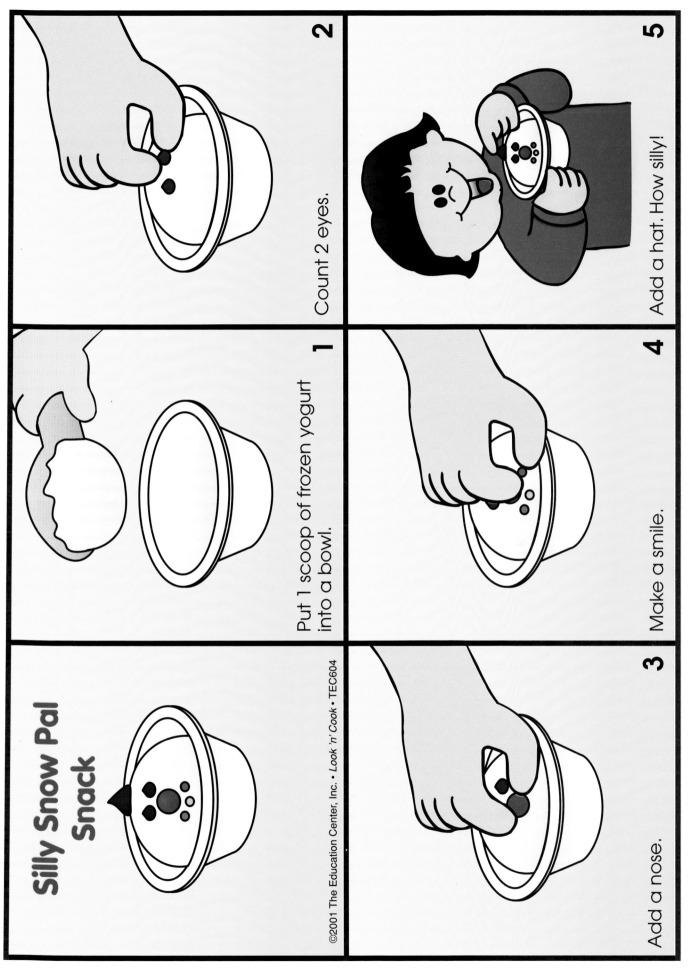

2

Count 2 eyes.

5

Add a hat. How silly!

1

Put 1 scoop of frozen yogurt into a bowl.

4

Make a smile.

Silly Snow Pal Snack

©2001 The Education Center, Inc. • *Look 'n' Cook* • TEC604

3

Add a nose.

Silly Snow Pal Snack

We are going to create a chilly snack! To help with this cooking project, please send in the item indicated below by _____. Thanks for making your child's learning fun and exciting!

___ container of vanilla frozen yogurt

___ bag of chocolate chips

___ jar of maraschino cherries

___ bag of M&M's® Minis® baking bits

___ large bag of Hershey's® Kisses® candies (plain)

___ package of disposable bowls

___ package of plastic spoons

___ package of napkins

I made a **Silly Snow Pal Snack** in school today!

My favorite part was _____.

It tasted _____.

This is what it looked like:

Chef's signature _____

An extra helping: Celebrate snow by reading *Snip, Snip…Snow!* by Nancy Poydar. Let it snow!

Hibernation Creation

These healthy bear snacks will have your little ones feeling toasty! No more growling tummies!

Ingredients for one:
1 slice of sandwich bread
peanut butter
3 banana slices
10 raisins

Utensils and supplies:
2 plastic bowls
toaster
1 plastic knife per child
napkins

Teacher preparation:
- Cut the bananas into slices. If desired, gently toss each slice in diluted lemon juice or lemon-lime soda to prevent browning. Then put the slices in a bowl.
- Put the raisins in a bowl.
- Arrange the ingredients and supplies near the step-by-step direction cards.
- Help students toast the bread as needed.

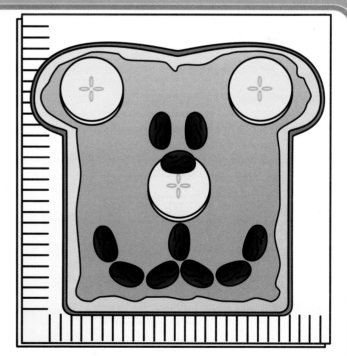

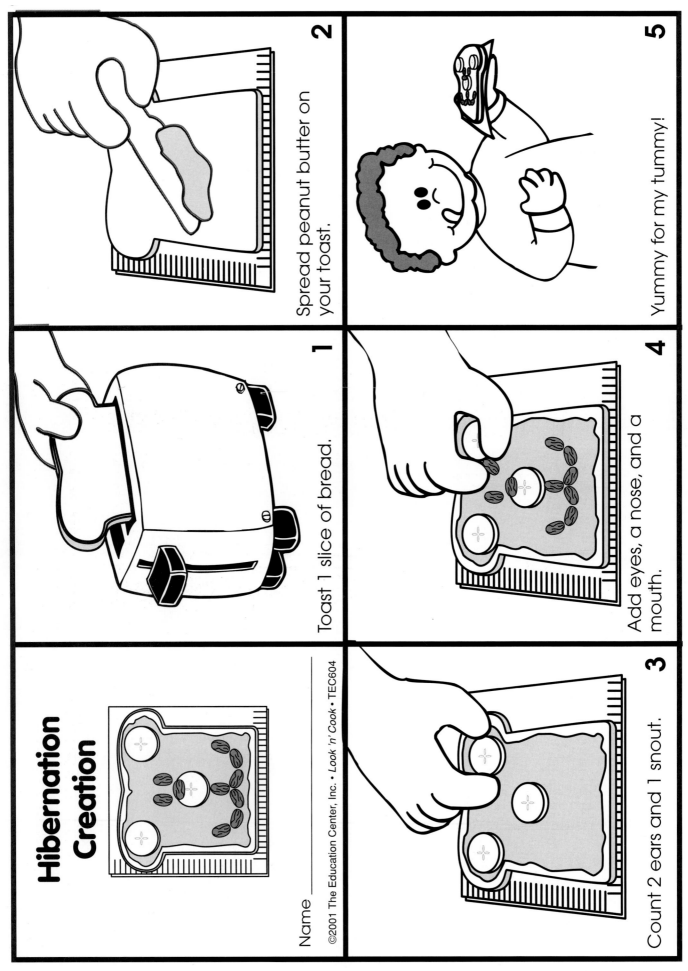

2

Spread peanut butter on your toast.

5

Yummy for my tummy!

1

Toast 1 slice of bread.

4

Add eyes, a nose, and a mouth.

Hibernation Creation

Name _____

©2001 The Education Center, Inc. • *Look 'n' Cook* • TEC604

3

Count 2 ears and 1 snout.

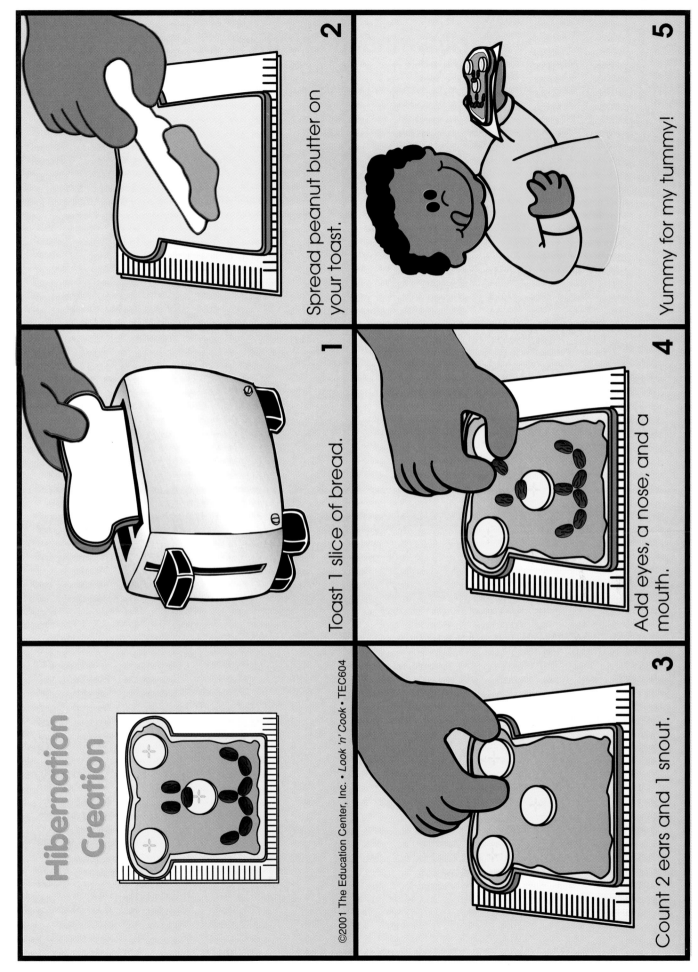

2 Spread peanut butter on your toast.

5 Yummy for my tummy!

1 Toast 1 slice of bread.

4 Add eyes, a nose, and a mouth.

Hibernation Creation

©2001 The Education Center, Inc. • *Look 'n' Cook* • TEC604

3 Count 2 ears and 1 snout.

Hibernation Creation

We are planning to make scrumptious bear snacks, and it's guaranteed that *these* bears won't be hibernating! To help us with this cooking project, please send in the item indicated below by _____. Thanks for making your child's learning fun and exciting!

___ loaf of sandwich bread

___ jar of peanut butter

___ several ripe bananas

___ large box of raisins

___ package of napkins

___ package of plastic knives

I made a **Hibernation Creation** in school today!

My favorite part was _____.

It tasted _____.

This is what it looked like:

Chef's signature _____

An extra helping: Learn more about hibernation and bears by reading *Every Autumn Comes the Bear* by Jim Arnosky.

Snowy Igloo

These incredible igloos will get your little ones enthused about the Arctic!

Ingredients for one:
1 scoop of ice cream (any flavor)
1 flat-bottomed ice-cream cone
 whipped topping

Utensils and supplies:
ice-cream scoop
1 paper plate per child
1 plastic knife per child
1 plastic spoon per child
napkins

Teacher preparation:
• Allow ice cream to soften slightly.
• Arrange the ingredients and supplies near the step-by-step direction cards.

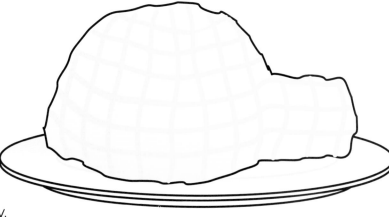

Snowy Igloo

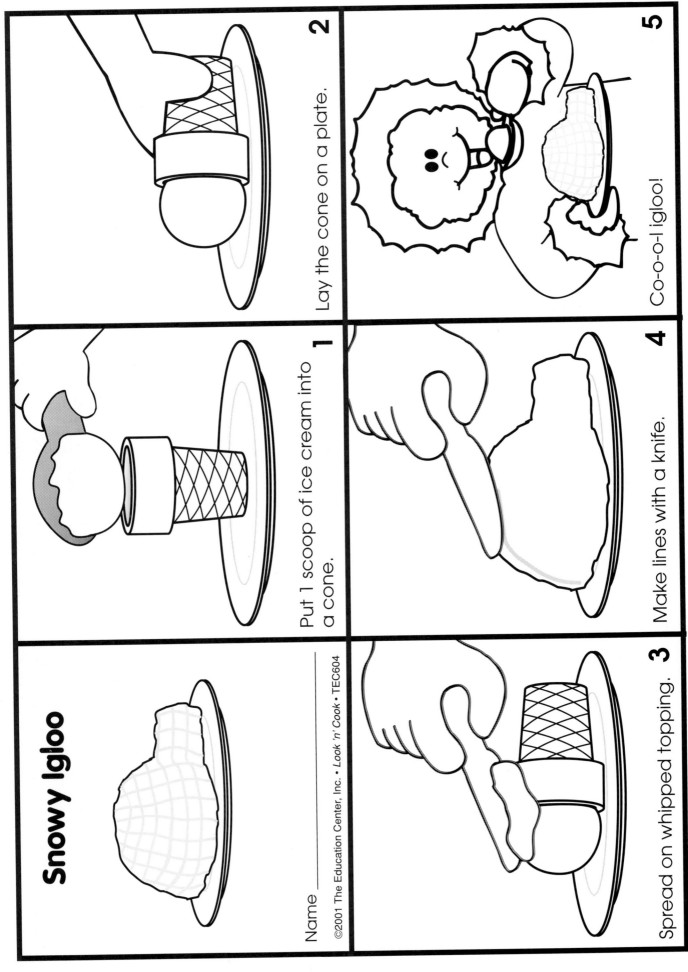

Name _____

©2001 The Education Center, Inc. • Look 'n' Cook • TEC604

1 Put 1 scoop of ice cream into a cone.

2 Lay the cone on a plate.

3 Spread on whipped topping.

4 Make lines with a knife.

5 Co-o-o-l igloo!

Snowy Igloo

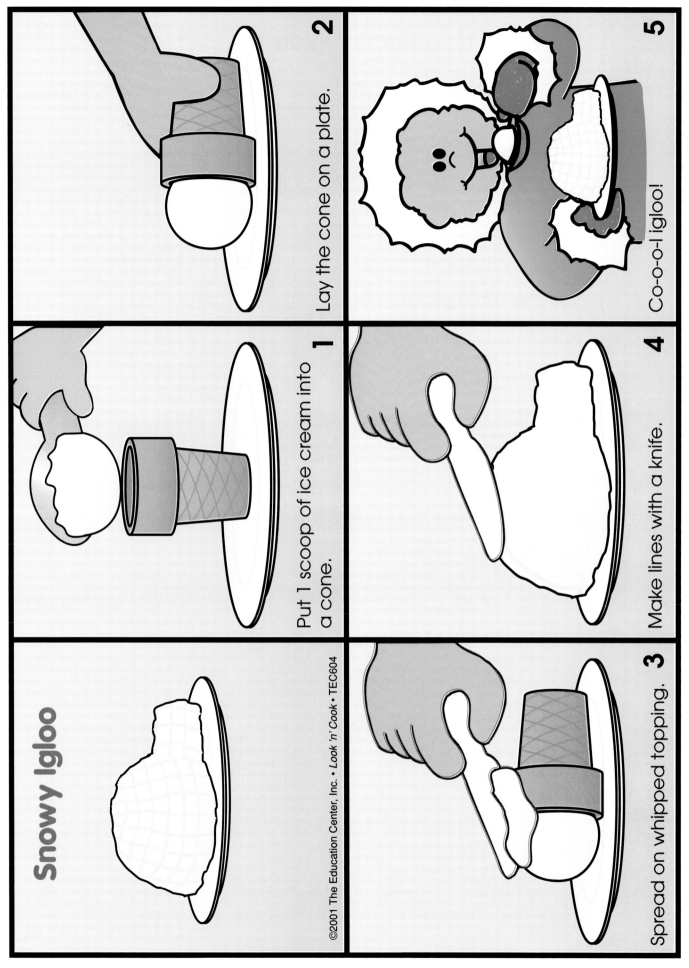

2 Lay the cone on a plate.

1 Put 1 scoop of ice cream into a cone.

5 Co-o-o-l igloo!

4 Make lines with a knife.

3 Spread on whipped topping.

Snowy Igloo

Our class is going to follow a simple recipe to make igloos that are good enough to eat! To help us with this cooking project, please send in the item indicated below by _____. Thanks for making your child's learning fun and exciting!

___ container of _____ ice cream

___ box of flat-bottomed ice-cream cones

___ package of paper plates

___ package of plastic knives

___ package of plastic spoons

___ package of napkins

I made a **Snowy Igloo** in school today!

My favorite part was _____.

It tasted _____.

This is what it looked like:

Chef's signature _____

An extra helping: Cozy up and read *Building an Igloo* by Ulli Steltzer. You'll be amazed to learn how real igloos are made!

Snowbird Snack

Most likely, you have a variety of winter birds right outside your classroom window! Invite your youngsters to discuss winter birds, and then have them make this tasty snack.

Ingredients for one:
1 graham cracker sheet
marshmallow fluff (snow)
5 raisins (birds)
5 mini chocolate chips (beaks)
sunflower seeds, shelled (birdseed)

Utensils and supplies:
3 plastic bowls
1 plastic knife per child
 napkins

Teacher preparation:
• Arrange the ingredients and supplies
  near the step-by-step direction cards.

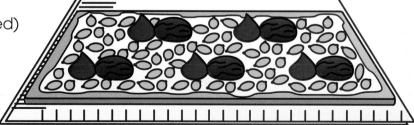

Snowbird Snack

2

Spread on some snow.

5

Feed the birds!

1

Put 1 graham cracker on the napkin.

Name _____

4

Give each bird a beak.

3

Count 5 birds.

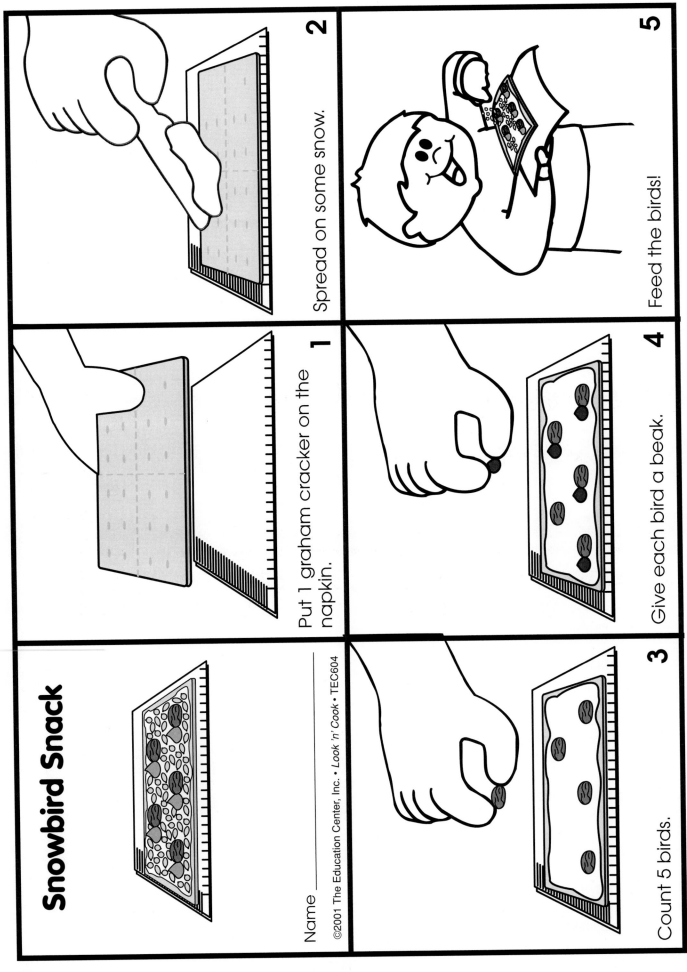

Snowbird Snack

2 Spread on some snow.

5 Feed the birds!

1 Put 1 graham cracker on the napkin.

©2001 The Education Center, Inc. • *Look 'n' Cook* • TEC604

4 Give each bird a beak.

3 Count 5 birds.

Snowbird Snack

Bird watching is a great winter activity! In school, we will be making Snowbird Snacks. To help us with this cooking project, please send in the item indicated below by _____. Thanks for making your child's learning fun and exciting!

___ box of graham crackers

___ jar of marshmallow fluff

___ large box of raisins

___ bag of mini chocolate chips

___ bag of shelled sunflower seeds

___ package of plastic knives

___ package of napkins

I made a **Snowbird Snack** in school today!

My favorite part was _____.

It tasted _____.

This is what it looked like:

Chef's signature _____

An extra helping: Want to learn more about our feathered friends? Check out the book *Feathers for Lunch* by Lois Ehlert!

Veggie Snowman

Here's a healthy snack idea that will have your little ones excited about snow!

Ingredients for one:
1 large round cracker
1 small round cracker
diced fresh vegetables
cream cheese (plain)

Utensils and supplies:
several bowls
1 plastic knife per child
napkins

Teacher preparation:
• Allow the cream cheese to soften.
• Dice the vegetables into small pieces and place each type in a separate bowl.
• Arrange the ingredients and supplies near the step-by-step direction cards.

Veggie Snowman

Name _____

©2001 The Education Center, Inc. • Look 'n' Cook • TEC604

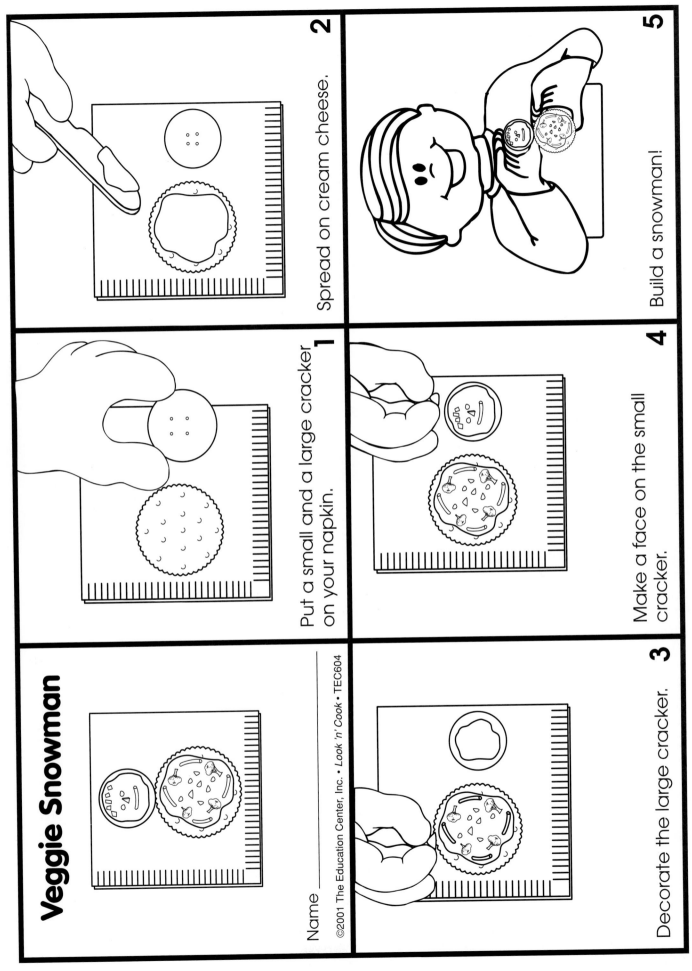

2 Spread on cream cheese.

5 Build a snowman!

1 Put a small and a large cracker on your napkin.

4 Make a face on the small cracker.

3 Decorate the large cracker.

Veggie Snowman

2 Spread on cream cheese.

5 Build a snowman!

1 Put a small and a large cracker on your napkin.

4 Make a face on the small cracker.

3 Decorate the large cracker.

Veggie Snowman

It wouldn't be winter without snowmen—so we're going to eat a few!
To help us with this cooking project, please send in the item indicated
below by _____. Thanks for making your child's learning fun and
exciting!

___ box of large round crackers

___ box of small round crackers

___ tub of plain cream cheese

___ fresh vegetable: _____

___ package of plastic knives

___ package of napkins

©2001 The Education Center, Inc. • *Look 'n' Cook* • TEC604

I made a **Veggie Snowman** in school today!

My favorite part was _____.

It tasted _____.

This is what it looked like:

Chef's signature _____

An extra helping: For a beautiful, colorful book about winter,
Check out *Snowballs* by Lois Ehlert on your next visit to the
library!

©2001 The Education Center, Inc. • *Look 'n' Cook* • TEC604

New Year's Slurpie

Add punch to the new year by having your little ones make this frosty, bubbly drink!

Ingredients for one:
1 tsp. frozen pink lemonade concentrate
ginger ale
1 scoop of rainbow sherbet
3 frozen strawberries
rainbow sprinkles in a shaker

Utensils and supplies:
1 bowl
ice-cream scoop
1 teaspoon
1 spoon
1 8-oz. clear plastic cup for each child
1 plastic spoon per child
1 straw per child
napkins

Teacher preparation:
- Allow the sherbet to soften slightly.
- Allow the frozen concentrate to thaw slightly.
- Put the strawberries in a bowl with the spoon.
- Arrange the ingredients and supplies near the step-by-step direction cards.

New Year's Slurpie

2 Add 1 scoop of sherbet.

5 Slurp! Happy new year!

1 Measure the lemonade.

4 Count 3 strawberries. Add sprinkles.

RAINBOW SPRINKLES

1 teaspoon

3 Add some ginger ale and stir.

Name _____

New Year's Slurpie

2 Add 1 scoop of sherbet.

5 Slurp! Happy new year!

1 Measure the lemonade.

4 Count 3 strawberries. Add sprinkles.

RAINBOW SPRINKLES

3 Add some ginger ale and stir.

New Year's Slurpie

After the holidays, we will be making tasty slurpies to ring in the new year. To help us with this cooking project, please send in the item indicated below by _____. Thanks for making your child's learning fun and exciting!

___ can frozen pink lemonade concentrate

___ container of rainbow sherbet

___ package of frozen strawberries

___ liter of ginger ale

___ container of rainbow sprinkles

___ package of 8-oz. clear plastic cups

___ package of straws

___ package of plastic spoons

___ package of napkins

I made a **New Year's Slurpie** in school today!

My favorite part was _____.

It tasted _____.

This is what it looked like:

Chef's signature _____

An extra helping: Find out how one particular polar bear celebrates New Year's by reading *P. Bear's New Year's Party: A Counting Book* by Paul Owen Lewis. Then count down to your own celebration!

Polar Bear Bite

Don't "paws" for a moment—take a bite out of winter with these scrumptious polar treats!

Ingredients for one:
1 scoop of vanilla ice cream
2 vanilla wafers (ears)
Reddi-wip® whipped cream (snout)
3 chocolate chips (eyes and nose)
two 2" two-inch pieces of red string licorice (mouth)

Utensils and supplies:
ice-cream scoop
1 paper plate per child
1 plastic spoon per child
napkins

Teacher preparation:
• Cut string licorice into two-inch pieces.
• Allow ice cream to soften slightly.
• Arrange the ingredients and supplies near the step-by-step direction cards.

Polar Bear Bite

Name _____

1 Put 1 scoop of ice cream on your plate.

2 Count 2 ears.

3 Squirt whipped cream to make a snout.

4 Make a bear face.

5 Take a bite—brrr!

Polar Bear Bite

1 Put 1 scoop of ice cream on your plate.

2 Count 2 ears.

3 Squirt whipped cream to make a snout.

4 Make a bear face.

5 Take a bite—brrr!

©2001 The Education Center, Inc. • *Look 'n' Cook* • TEC604

79

Polar Bear Bite

We will be making some delicious Arctic masterpieces in school! To help us with this cooking project, please send in the item indicated below by _____. Thanks for making your child's learning fun and exciting!

___ container of vanilla ice cream

___ large box of vanilla wafers

___ Reddi-wip® whipped cream

___ bag of chocolate chips

___ package of red string licorice

___ package of paper plates

___ package of napkins

___ package of plastic spoons

I made a **Polar Bear Bite** in school today!

My favorite part was _____.

It tasted _____.

This is what it looked like:

Chef's signature _____

An extra helping: For fun reading, look up *Little Polar Bear and the Brave Little Hare* by Hans de Beer on your next trip to the library!

Gumdrop Groundhog

Great groundhogs! February 2 is approaching! These unique creations will be nibbled before they get a chance to cast shadows!

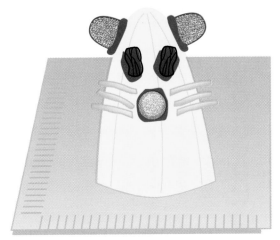

Ingredients for one:
2" end of unpeeled banana
chocolate frosting
2 raisins (eyes)
3 gumdrops or spice drops (ears and nose)
6 chow mein noodles (whiskers)

Utensils and supplies:
1 plastic knife per child
napkins

Teacher preparation:
• Cut each banana two inches from both ends. Do not peel.
• Arrange the ingredients and supplies near the step-by-step direction cards.

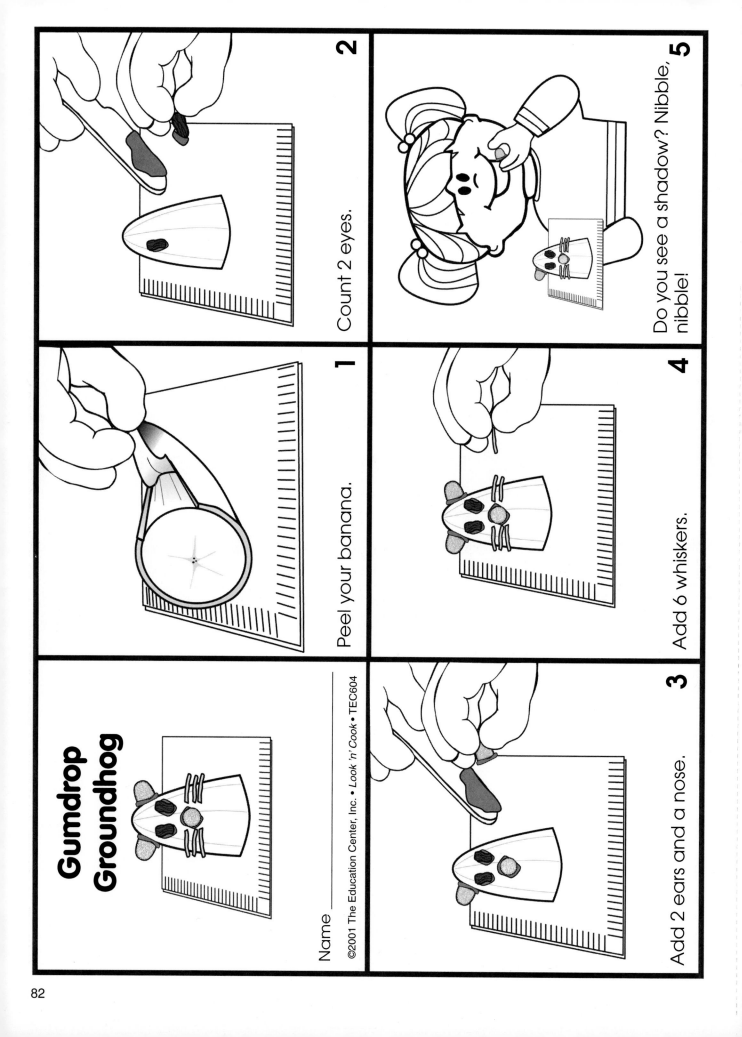

2

Count 2 eyes.

5

Do you see a shadow? Nibble, nibble!

1

Peel your banana.

4

Add 6 whiskers.

Gumdrop Groundhog

Name _____

©2001 The Education Center, Inc. • *Look 'n' Cook* • TEC604

3

Add 2 ears and a nose.

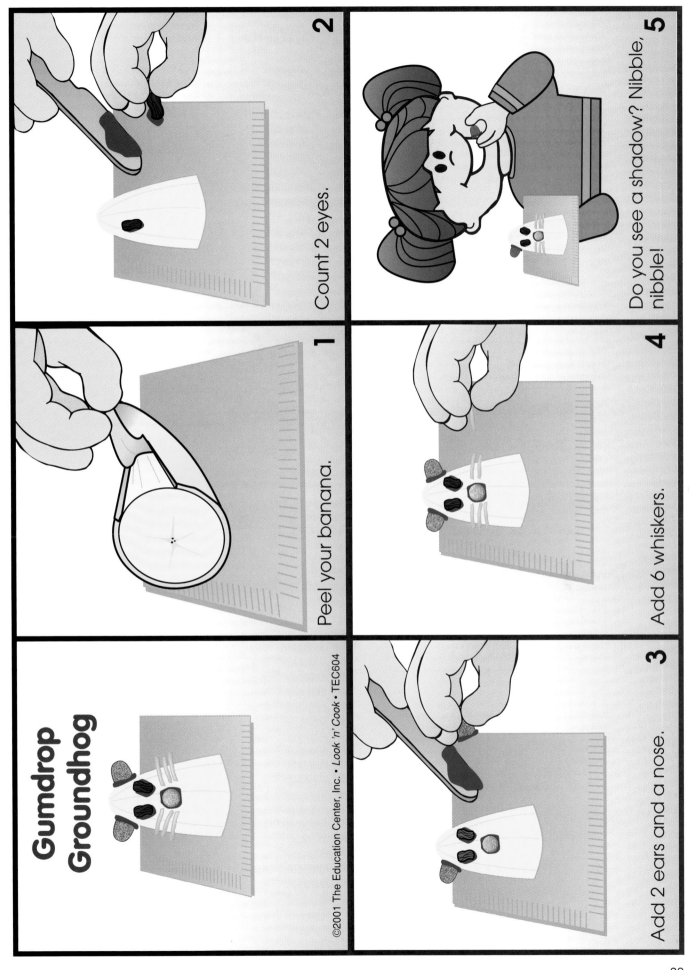

2

Count 2 eyes.

5

Do you see a shadow? Nibble, nibble!

1

Peel your banana.

4

Add 6 whiskers.

©2001 The Education Center, Inc. • Look 'n' Cook • TEC604

Gumdrop Groundhog

3

Add 2 ears and a nose.

Gumdrop Groundhog

Will the groundhog see his shadow on Groundhog Day? We'll have to wait and see, but we're certain there will be cooking excitement in our classroom! To help us with this project, please send in the item indicated below by _____. Thanks for making your child's learning fun and exciting!

___ bananas

___ box of raisins

___ large bag of small gumdrops or spice drops

___ container of chow mein noodles

___ can of chocolate frosting

___ package of napkins

___ package of plastic knives

I made a **Gumdrop Groundhog** in school today!

My favorite part was _____.

It tasted _____.

This is what it looked like:

Chef's signature _____

An extra helping: Will Geoffrey see his shadow? Read *Geoffrey Groundhog Predicts the Weather* by Bruce Koscielniak to find out!

Sweet Surprise

Add some love to your Valentine's Day party with these cute cupcakes!

BE MINE

CUTIE PIE

Bessie

Ingredients for one:
vanilla cupcake batter
1 Hershey's® Kisses® candy
vanilla frosting
red and white candy sprinkles

Utensils and supplies:
1 foil cupcake liner per child
permanent marker
1 spoon
red food coloring
bowl
oven
1 plastic knife per child
napkins

Teacher preparation:
• Personalize a foil cupcake liner for each child.
• Use your favorite recipe to prepare a batch of vanilla cupcake batter.
• Tint the frosting pink with red food coloring.
• Unwrap a class supply of Hershey's Kisses candies and place them in a bowl.
• Arrange the ingredients and supplies near the step-by-step direction cards.
• Bake the cupcakes according to your recipe.

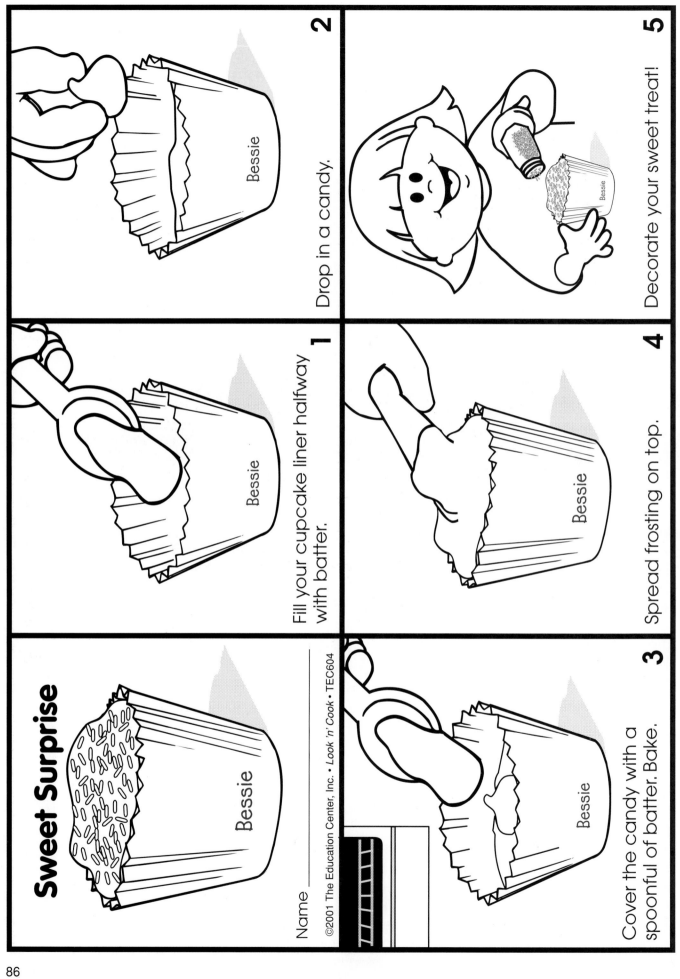

Sweet Surprise

Bessie

Name _____

©2001 The Education Center, Inc. • *Look 'n' Cook* • TEC604

2

Bessie

Drop in a candy.

5

Bessie

Decorate your sweet treat!

1

Bessie

Fill your cupcake liner halfway with batter.

4

Bessie

Spread frosting on top.

3

Bessie

Cover the candy with a spoonful of batter. Bake.

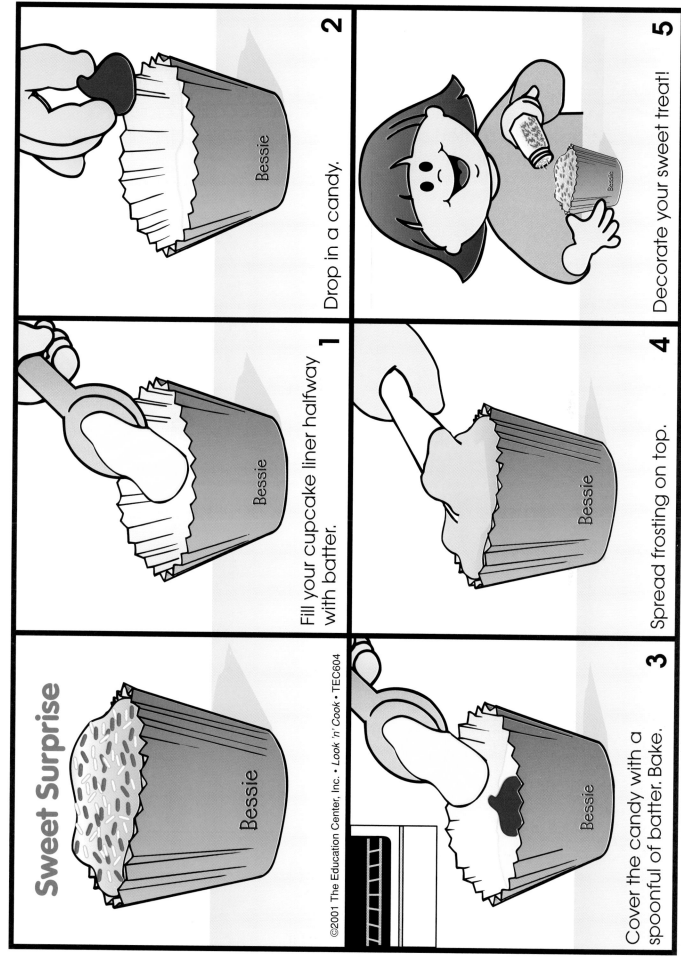

Sweet Surprise

2 Drop in a candy.

5 Decorate your sweet treat!

1 Fill your cupcake liner halfway with batter.

4 Spread frosting on top.

3 Cover the candy with a spoonful of batter. Bake.

©2001 The Education Center, Inc. • *Look 'n' Cook* • TEC604

Sweet Surprise

Valentine's Day is a time to show friends and loved ones that you care about them. We are going to work together to make special cupcakes with chocolate treats inside! To help us with this cooking project, please send in the item indicated below by _____. Thanks for making your child's learning fun and exciting!

___ large bag of Hershey's® Kisses® candies

___ can of vanilla frosting

___ red and white candy sprinkles

___ foil cupcake liners

___ package of food coloring

___ package of plastic knives

___ package of napkins

I made a **Sweet Surprise** in school today!

My favorite part was _____.

It tasted _____.

This is what it looked like:

Chef's signature _____

An extra helping: *Froggy's First Kiss* by Jonathan London is a story with a very sweet ending! Look it up at your local library and enjoy.

Hearts Aflutter

These cute critters will create lots of culinary excitement!

Ingredients for one:
2 slices of sandwich bread
strawberry jam
grape jelly
Froot Loops® cereal pieces (spots)
Two 1" lengths of red string licorice (antennae)

Utensils and supplies:
1 bowl
large heart-shaped cookie cutter
small heart-shaped cookie cutter
1 plastic knife per child
napkins

Teacher preparation:
• Cut string licorice into one-inch pieces and place in a bowl.
• Arrange the ingredients and supplies near the step-by-step direction cards.

Hearts Aflutter

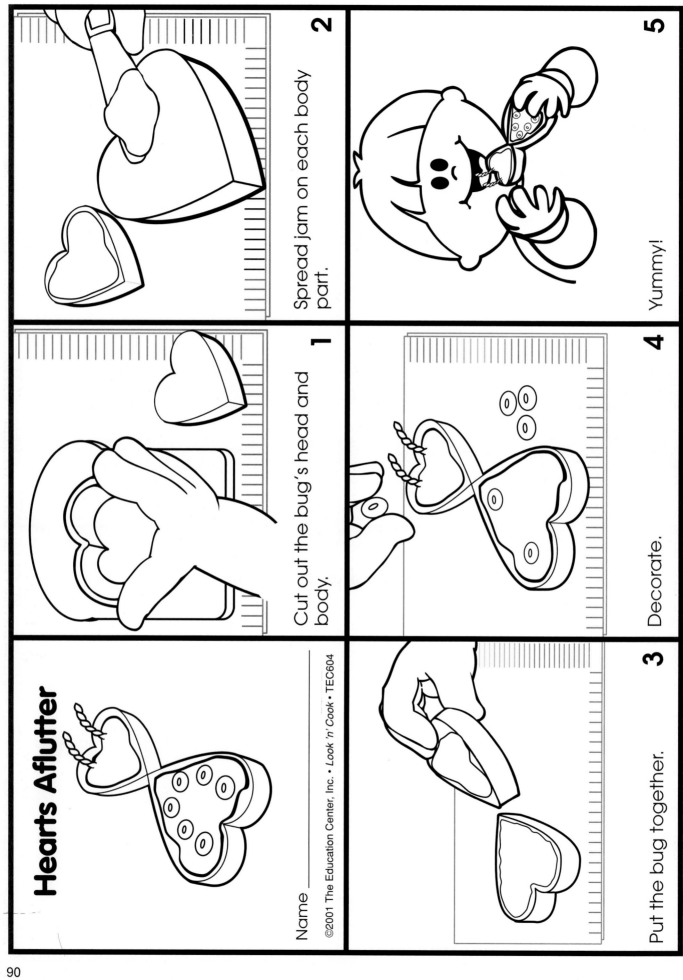

Name _____

1 Cut out the bug's head and body.

2 Spread jam on each body part.

3 Put the bug together.

4 Decorate.

5 Yummy!

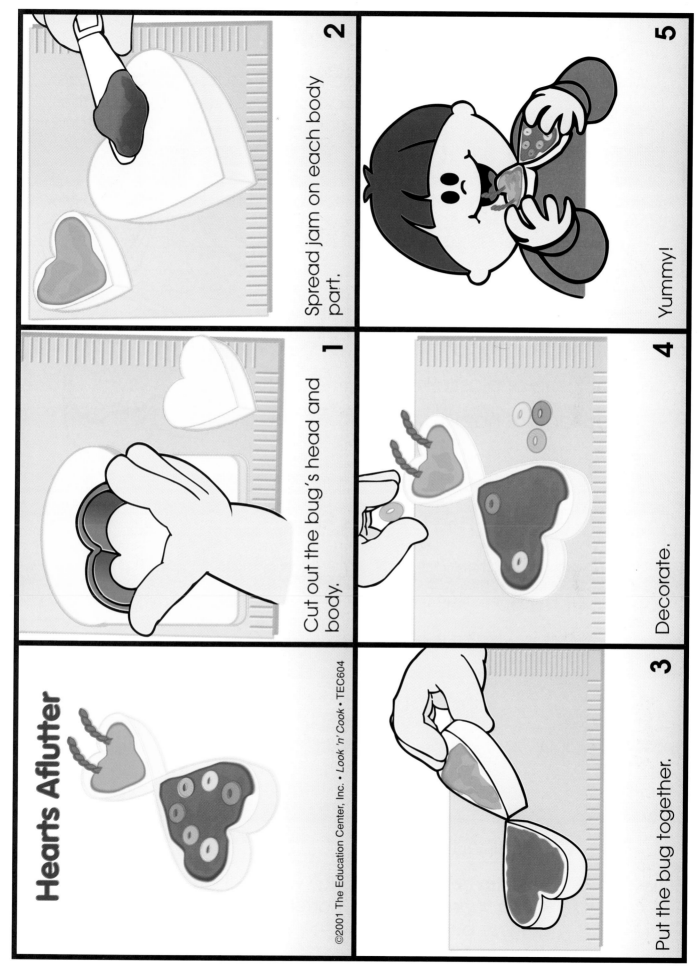

2 Spread jam on each body part.

5 Yummy!

1 Cut out the bug's head and body.

4 Decorate.

Hearts Aflutter

©2001 The Education Center, Inc. • *Look 'n' Cook* • TEC604

3 Put the bug together.

91

Hearts Aflutter

We're going to treat ourselves to some valentine fun by making lovely bugs for snack! To help us with this cooking project, please send in the item indicated below by _____. Thanks for making your child's learning fun and exciting!

___ loaf of sandwich bread

___ jar of strawberry jam

___ jar of grape jelly

___ box of Froot Loops® cereal

___ package of red string licorice

___ package of plastic knives

___ package of napkins

I made a **Hearts Aflutter bug** in school today!

My favorite part was _____.

It tasted _____.

This is what it looked like:

Chef's signature _____

An extra helping: Go buggy with the book *Alpha Bugs* by David A. Carter. Can you count all those bugs?

Friendship Hearts

Invite each child to make two Friendship Hearts—one for herself and one for a friend!

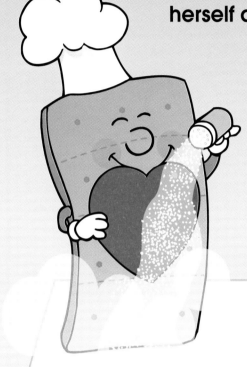

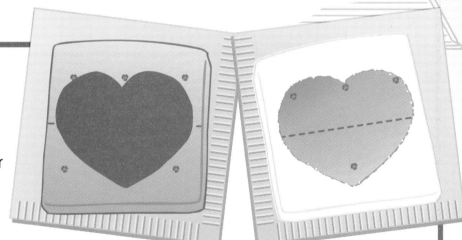

Ingredients for one:
1 graham cracker sheet
powdered sugar

Utensils and supplies:
red or pink construction paper
scissors
shaker for powdered sugar
napkins

Teacher preparation:
- Cut out small construction paper hearts that will fit on a graham cracker half.
- Fill the shaker with powdered sugar.
- Break each graham cracker sheet in half.
- Arrange the ingredients and supplies near the step-by-step direction cards.

Friendship Hearts

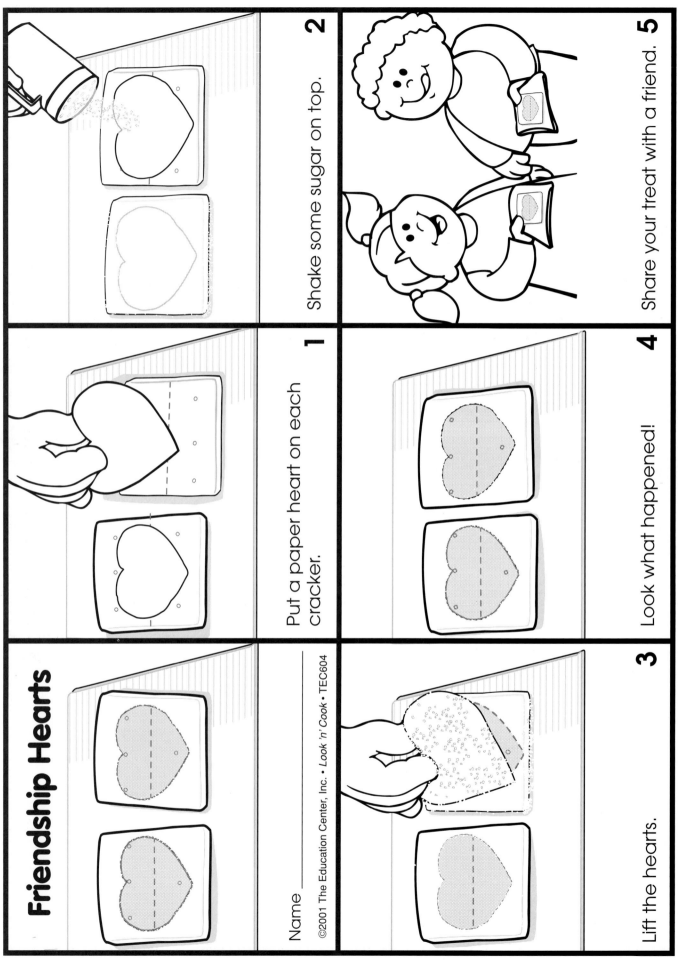

2 Shake some sugar on top.

5 Share your treat with a friend.

1 Put a paper heart on each cracker.

Name _____

©2001 The Education Center, Inc. • Look 'n' Cook • TEC604

4 Look what happened!

3 Lift the hearts.

94

Friendship Hearts

2 Shake some sugar on top.

1 Put a paper heart on each cracker.

©2001 The Education Center, Inc. • *Look 'n' Cook* • TEC604

5 Share your treat with a friend.

4 Look what happened!

3 Lift the hearts.

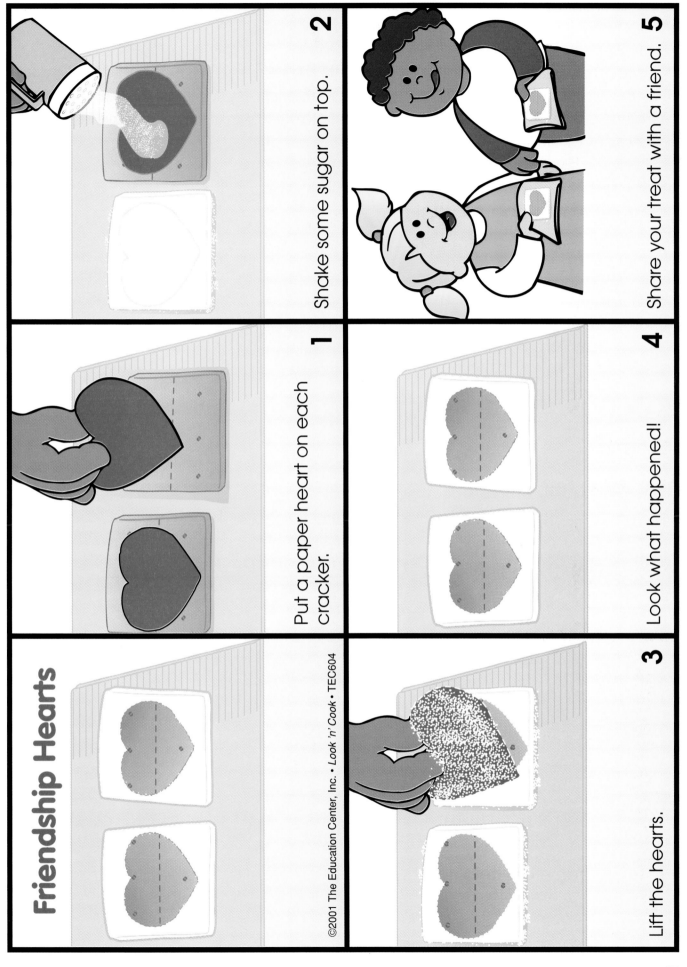

95

Friendship Hearts

Hearts, hearts, hearts! We're going to share some tasty heart cookies with our friends. To help us with this cooking project, please send in the item indicated below by _____. Thanks for making your child's learning fun and exciting!

___ box of graham crackers

___ bag or box of powdered sugar

___ package of napkins

I made **Friendship Hearts** in school today!

My favorite part was _____.

It tasted _____.

This is what it looked like:

Chef's signature _____

An extra helping: Share the book *Franklin's Valentines* by Paulette Bourgeois with your child. Love is what it's all about!

Lincoln's Log Cabin

Stick to this cooking idea that will build your youngsters' enthusiasm for creative snacks!

Ingredients for one:
1 slice of sandwich bread
5 thin pretzel sticks (logs)
honey in a squeeze bottle

Utensils and supplies:
toaster
napkins

Teacher preparation:
• Arrange the ingredients and supplies near the step-by-step direction cards.

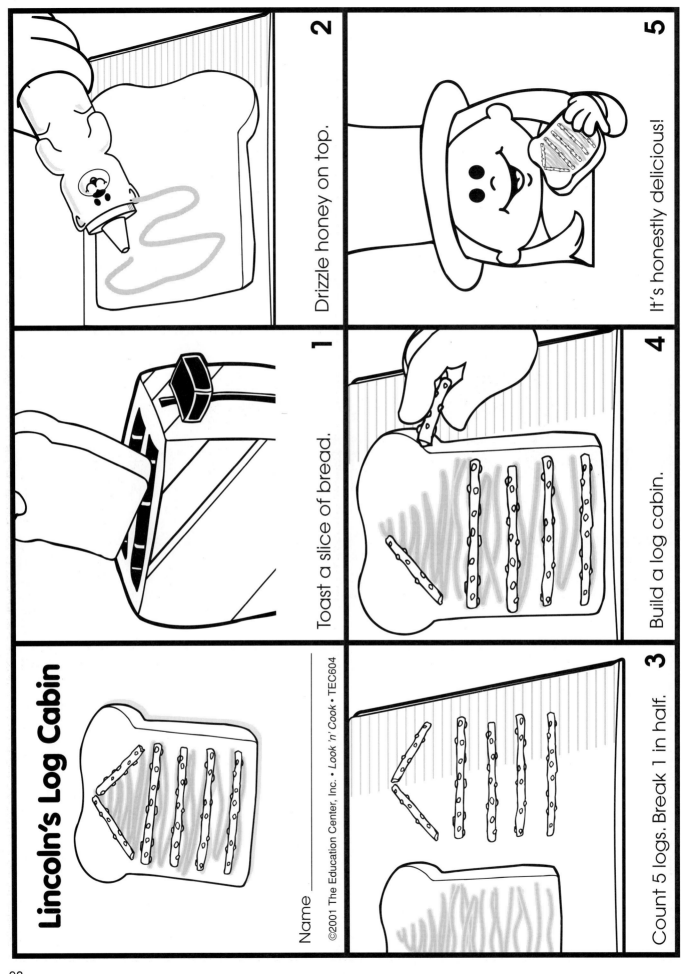

Lincoln's Log Cabin

Name _____

1 Toast a slice of bread.

2 Drizzle honey on top.

3 Count 5 logs. Break 1 in half.

4 Build a log cabin.

5 It's honestly delicious!

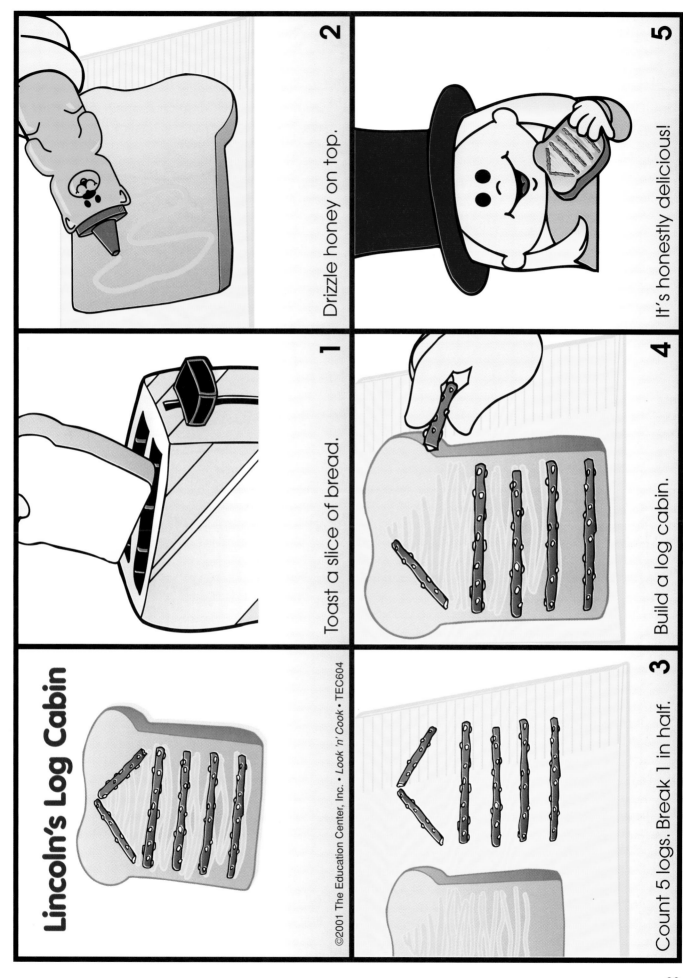

Lincoln's Log Cabin

1 Toast a slice of bread.

2 Drizzle honey on top.

3 Count 5 logs. Break 1 in half.

4 Build a log cabin.

5 It's honestly delicious!

©2001 The Education Center, Inc. • *Look 'n' Cook* • TEC604

99

Lincoln's Log Cabin

Our class "wood" like to make some edible log cabins to help celebrate Lincoln's birthday. To help us with this cooking project, please send in the item indicated below by _____. Thanks for making your child's learning fun and exciting!

___ loaf of sandwich bread

___ squeeze bottle of honey

___ large bag of thin pretzel sticks

___ package of napkins

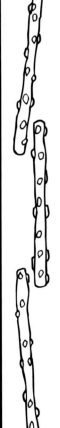

I made **Lincoln's Log Cabin** in school today!

My favorite part was _____.

It tasted _____.

This is what it looked like:

Chef's signature _____

An extra helping: To get a feel for what a log cabin is like, look for *Dance at Grandpa's* by Laura Ingalls Wilder the next time you visit your local library!

Kite Bite

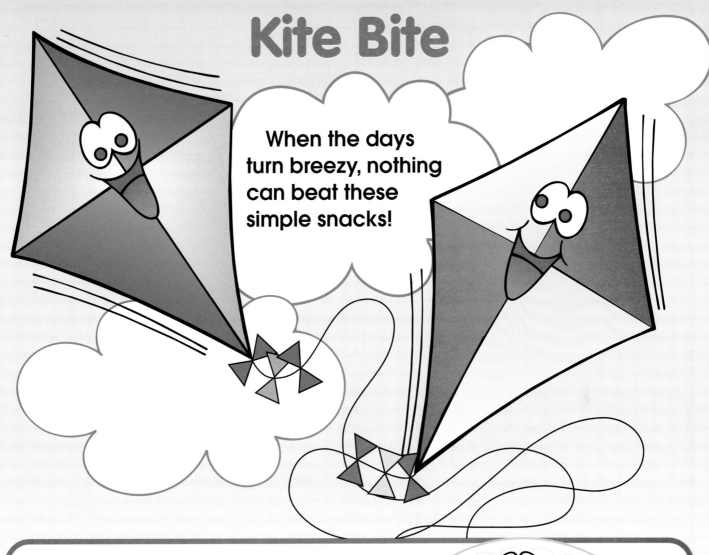

When the days turn breezy, nothing can beat these simple snacks!

Ingredients for one:
1 slice of sandwich bread
peanut butter
fruit-flavored cream cheese
grape jelly
strawberry jam
one 3" length of red string licorice
    (kite tail)

Utensils and supplies:
2 plastic plates
4 plastic knives
napkins

Teacher preparation:
- Cut the crust off each bread slice.
- Cut each slice into four triangular pieces by cutting twice diagonally. Put the triangles on a plate.
- Cut the string licorice into three-inch lengths to resemble kite tails; then put them on a plate.
- Arrange the ingredients and supplies near the step-by-step direction cards.

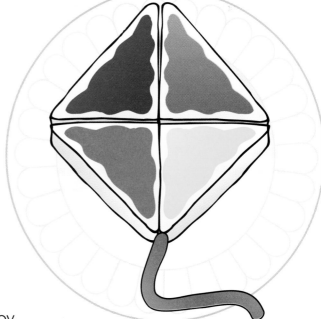

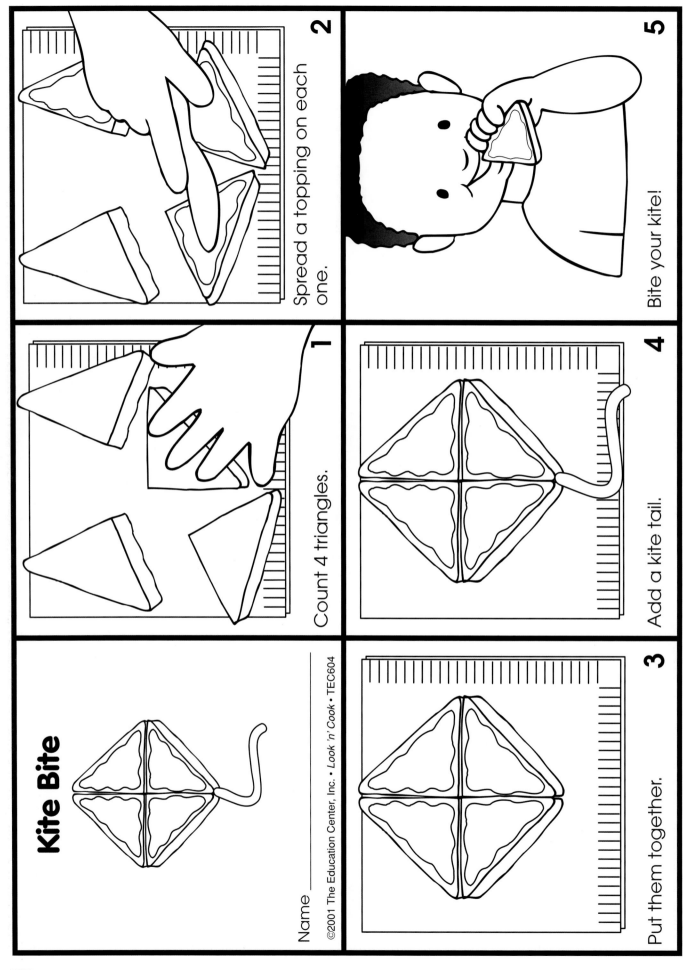

2

Spread a topping on each one.

5

Bite your kite!

1

Count 4 triangles.

4

Add a kite tail.

Kite Bite

Name

3

Put them together.

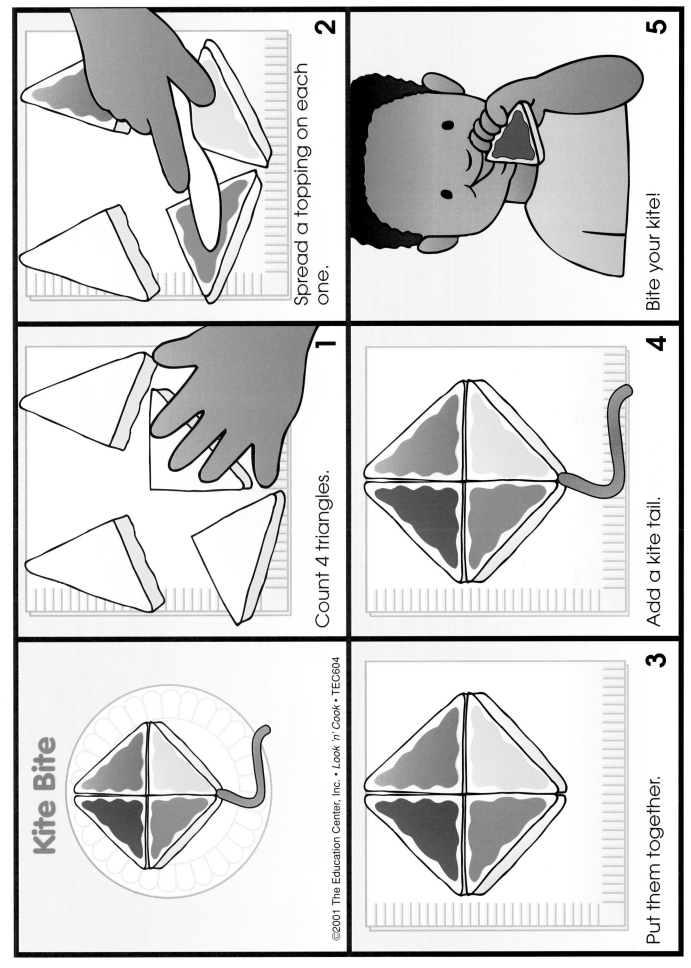

2

Spread a topping on each one.

5

Bite your kite!

1

Count 4 triangles.

4

Add a kite tail.

Kite Bite

©2001 The Education Center, Inc. • *Look 'n' Cook* • TEC604

3

Put them together.

Kite Bite

Windy days are upon us, so we're going to let our imaginations soar with some kite snacks! To help us with this cooking project, please send in the item indicated below by _____. Thanks for making your child's learning fun and exciting!

___ loaf of sandwich bread

___ tub of fruit-flavored cream cheese: _____

___ jar of peanut butter

___ jar of grape jelly

___ jar of strawberry jam

___ package of red string licorice

___ package of plastic knives

___ package of napkins

I made a **Kite Bite** in school today!

My favorite part was _____.

It tasted _____.

This is what it looked like:

Chef's signature _____

An extra helping: Fly away with *Catch the Wind! All About Kites* by Gail Gibbons. Kites are such fun!

Magical Shamrock Potion

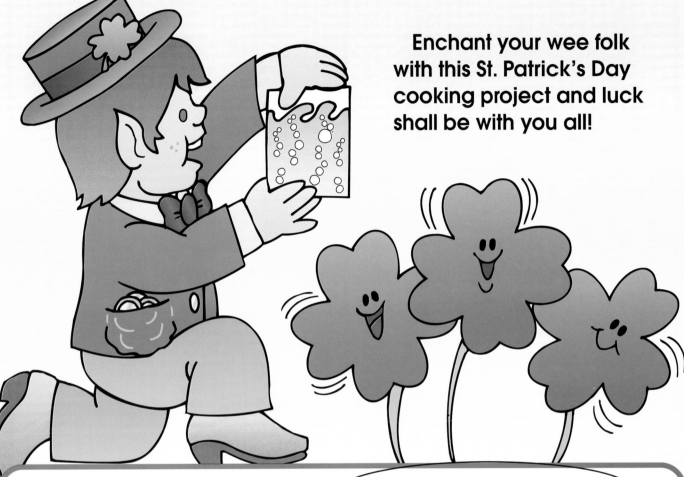

Enchant your wee folk with this St. Patrick's Day cooking project and luck shall be with you all!

Ingredients for one:
1 tsp. frozen lemonade concentrate
lime-flavored seltzer water
1 scoop of lime sherbet
3 Lucky Charms® marshmallows
rainbow sprinkles

Utensils and supplies:
plastic bowl
1 teaspoon
ice-cream scoop
one 8-oz. clear plastic cup per child
1 plastic spoon per child
napkins

Teacher preparation:
* Allow the sherbet to soften slightly.
* Allow the frozen concentrate to thaw slightly.
* Separate the marshmallows from a box of Lucky Charms® cereal; then put them in a bowl.
* Arrange the ingredients and supplies near the step-by-step direction cards.

Magical Shamrock Potion

Name _____

©2001 The Education Center, Inc. • Look 'n' Cook • TEC604

1 Measure the lemonade.

2 Add 1 scoop of sherbet.

3 Add seltzer water and stir.

4 Count 3 marshmallows. Add some magic sprinkles.

5 Drink up for good luck!

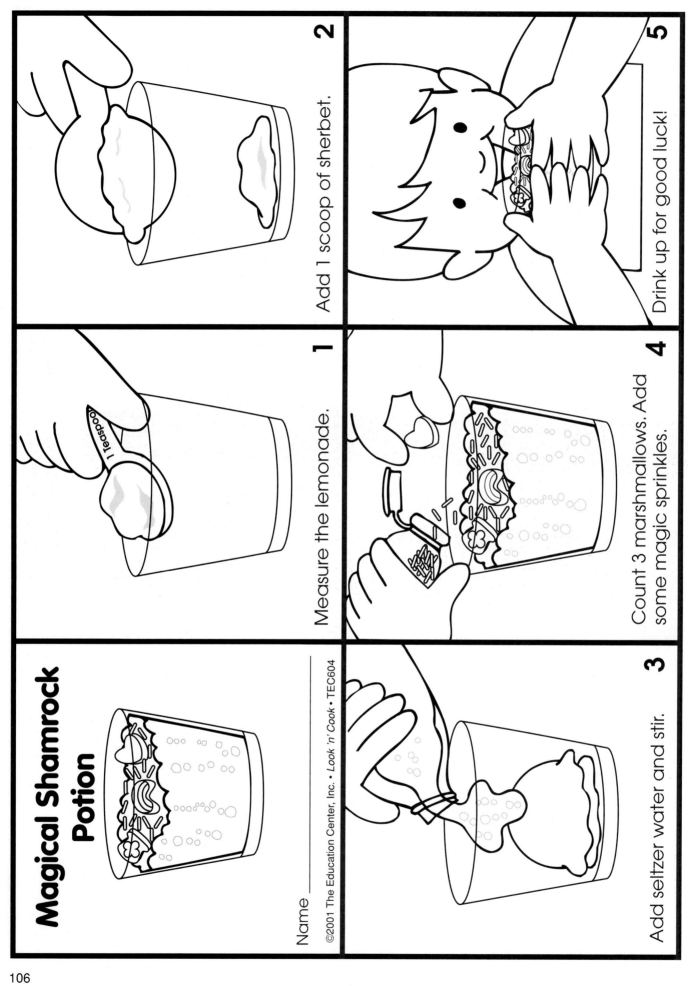

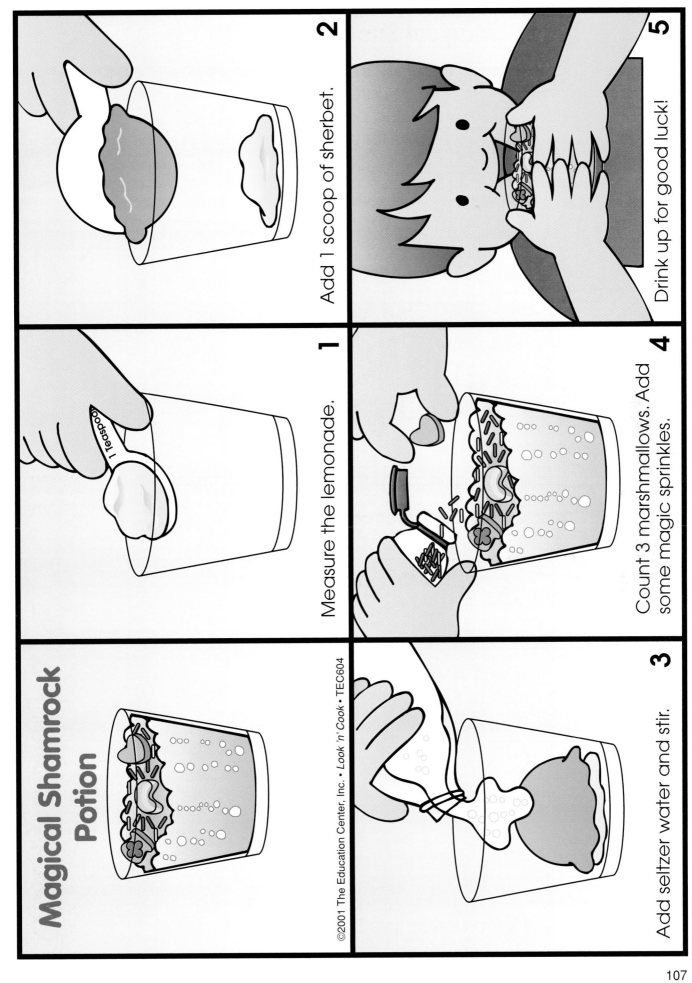

Magical Shamrock Potion

1 Measure the lemonade.

2 Add 1 scoop of sherbet.

3 Add seltzer water and stir.

4 Count 3 marshmallows. Add some magic sprinkles.

5 Drink up for good luck!

©2001 The Education Center, Inc. • *Look 'n' Cook* • TEC604

Magical Shamrock Potion

Leaping leprechauns! St. Patrick's Day is nearly upon us. To bring some good luck into our classroom, we are going to make Magical Shamrock Potion. To help us with this cooking project, please send in the item indicated below by_____. Thanks for making your child's learning fun and exciting!

___ can of frozen lemonade concentrate

___ container of lime sherbet

___ box of Lucky Charms® cereal

___ container of rainbow sprinkles

___ liter of lime-flavored seltzer water

___ package of 8-oz. clear plastic cups

___ package of plastic spoons

___ package of napkins

I made **Magical Shamrock Potion** in school today!

My favorite part was _____.

It tasted _____.

This is what it looked like:

Chef's signature _____

An extra helping: For a charming story, read *St. Patrick's Day in the Morning* by Eve Bunting.

Pot of Gold

What's a St. Paddy's Day party without a pot of gold? Your little ones will enjoy a wealth of good taste with this dessert!

Ingredients for one:
1 scoop of cookies-and-cream ice cream
6 banana slices (gold)
whipped topping

Utensils and supplies:
knife
plastic bowl
yellow food coloring
ice-cream scoop
one 8-oz. clear plastic cup per child
1 plastic spoon per child
napkins

Teacher preparation:
• Tint the whipped topping with yellow food coloring.
• Peel the bananas and then cut them into thin slices. If desired, toss the slices with diluted lemon juice or lemon-lime soda to prevent browning. Put the banana slices in a bowl.
• Allow the ice cream to soften slightly.
• Arrange the ingredients and supplies near the step-by-step direction cards.

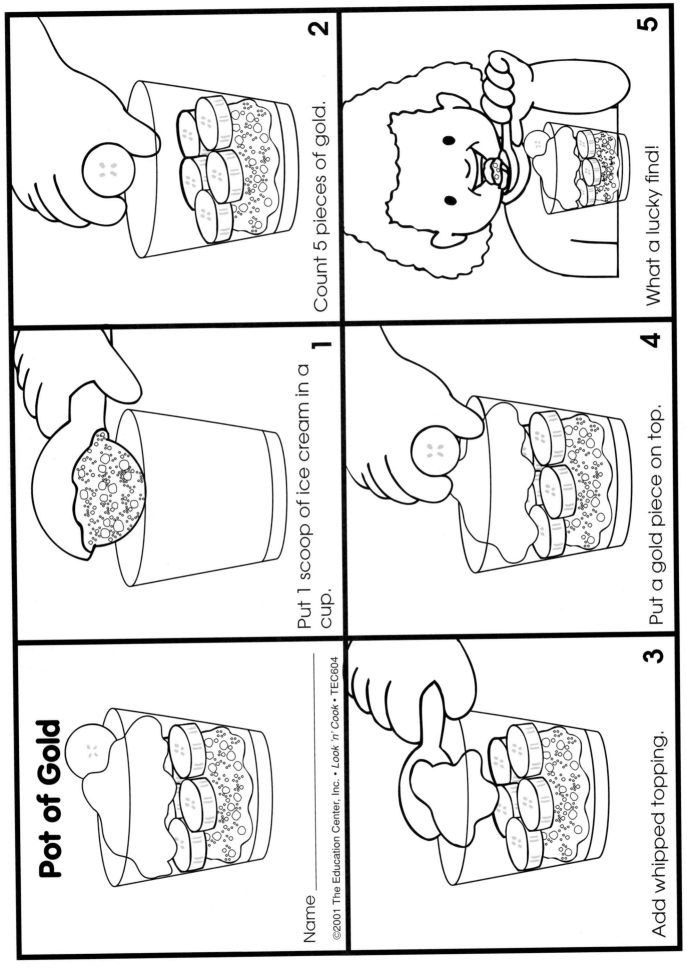

Pot of Gold

Name _____

©2001 The Education Center, Inc. • *Look 'n' Cook* • TEC604

1 Put 1 scoop of ice cream in a cup.

2 Count 5 pieces of gold.

3 Add whipped topping.

4 Put a gold piece on top.

5 What a lucky find!

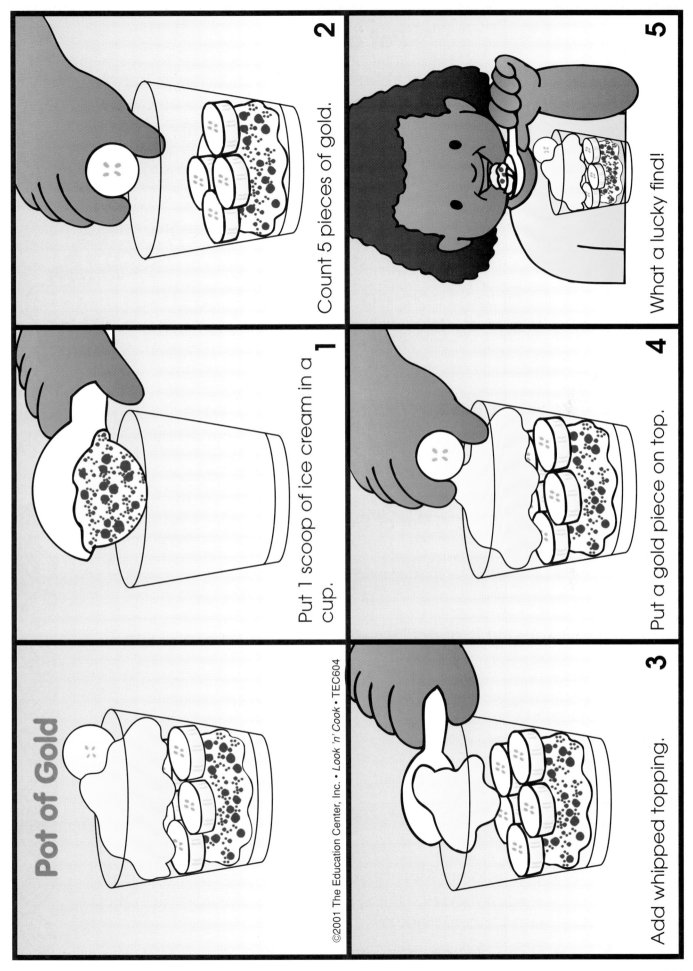

2

Count 5 pieces of gold.

5

What a lucky find!

1

Put 1 scoop of ice cream in a cup.

4

Put a gold piece on top.

Pot of Gold

©2001 The Education Center, Inc. • *Look 'n' Cook* • TEC604

3

Add whipped topping.

Pot of Gold

We're going to strike it rich when we make pots of gold! To help us with this cooking project, please send in the item indicated below by _____. Thanks for making your child's learning fun and exciting!

___ container of cookies-and-cream ice cream

___ bananas

___ container of whipped topping

___ package of food coloring

___ package of 8-oz. clear plastic cups

___ package of plastic spoons

___ package of napkins

I made a **Pot of Gold** in school today!

My favorite part was _____.

It tasted _____.

This is what it looked like:

Chef's signature _____

An extra helping: Stop at your local library to check out *The Gold at the End of the Rainbow* by Wolfram Hanel. You won't soon forget this story!

Eating a Rainbow

Spring brings many things! Discuss rainbows with your youngsters and then have them cook up a storm!

Ingredients for one:
1 graham cracker sheet
marshmallow fluff (clouds)
Fruity Pebbles® cereal (rainbow)

Utensils and supplies:
plastic bowl
1 plastic knife per child
napkins

Teacher preparation:
- Pour the cereal into the bowl.
- Arrange the ingredients and supplies near the step-by-step direction cards.

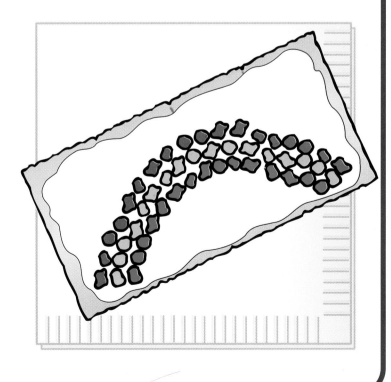

Eating a Rainbow

Name _____

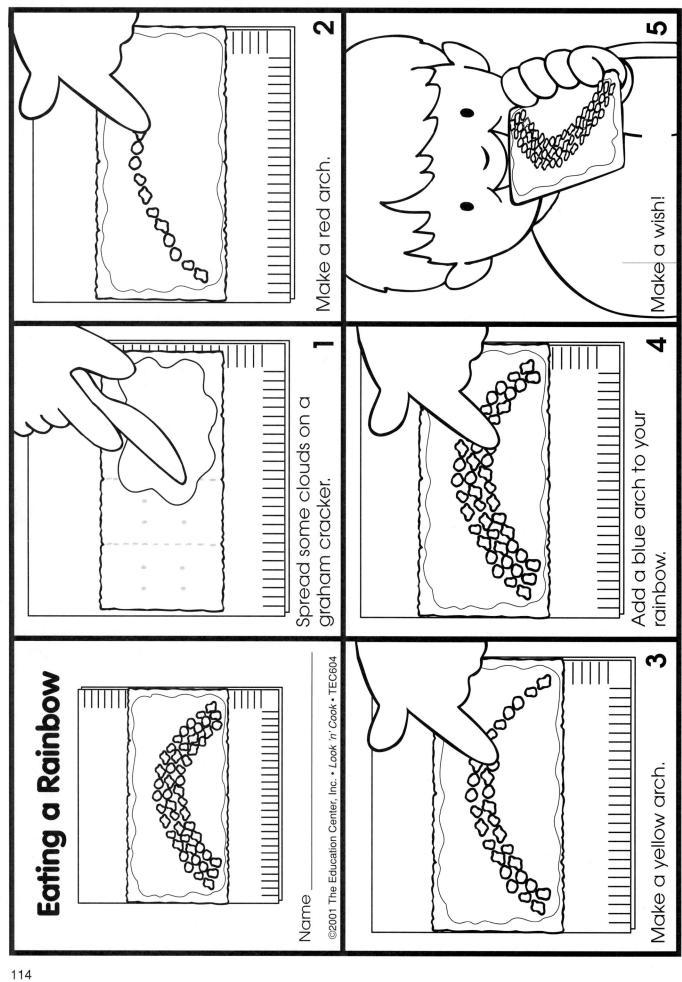

1 Spread some clouds on a graham cracker.

2 Make a red arch.

3 Make a yellow arch.

4 Add a blue arch to your rainbow.

5 Make a wish!

Eating a Rainbow

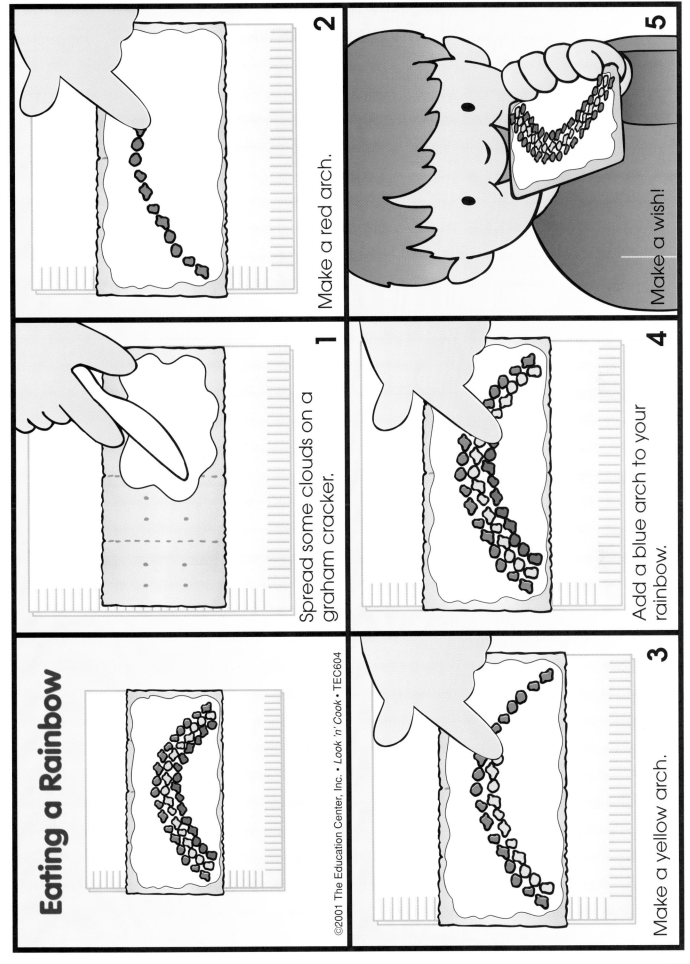

2 Make a red arch.

1 Spread some clouds on a graham cracker.

5 Make a wish!

4 Add a blue arch to your rainbow.

3 Make a yellow arch.

Eating a Rainbow

Red, orange, yellow, green, blue, and purple too—all these colors make a rainbow, it's true! Our class is going to make rainbow snacks. To help us with this cooking project, please send in the item indicated below by _____. Thanks for making your child's learning fun and exciting!

___ box of graham crackers

___ jar of marshmallow fluff

___ box of Fruity Pebbles® cereal

___ package of plastic knives

___ package of napkins

I **ate a Rainbow** in school today!

My favorite part was _____.

It tasted _____.

This is what it looked like:

Chef's signature _____

An extra helping: Read *Planting a Rainbow* by Lois Ehlert. Rainbows come in many types and sizes!

Peanut Butter Pinwheel

Round and round the pinwheel goes! Try these creative snacks with your youngsters for a whirl of cooking excitement.

Ingredients for one:
2 slices of sandwich bread
1 red licorice stick (handle)
peanut butter

Utensils and supplies:
1 plastic knife per child
napkins

Teacher preparation:
• Arrange the ingredients and supplies near the step-by-step direction cards.

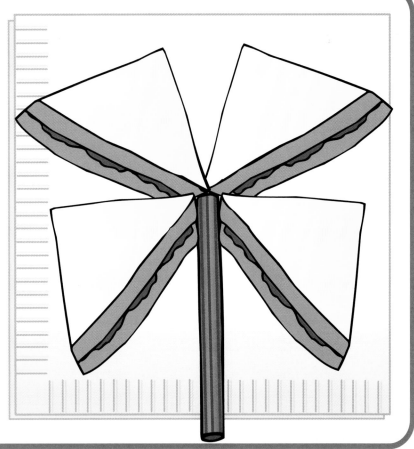

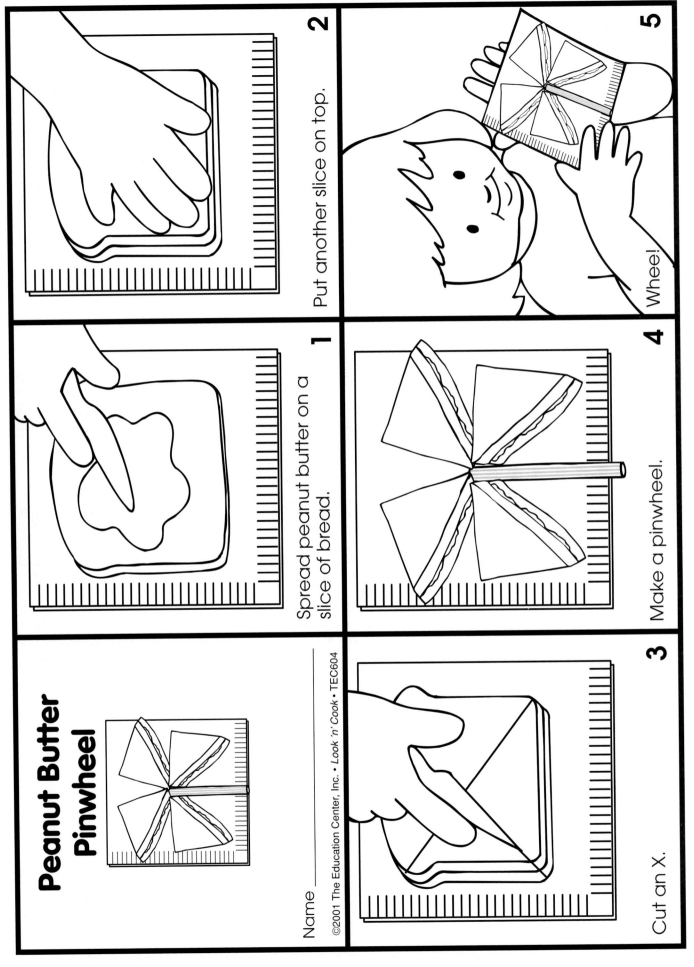

Peanut Butter Pinwheel

Name _____

2 Put another slice on top.

1 Spread peanut butter on a slice of bread.

5 Whee!

4 Make a pinwheel.

3 Cut an X.

©2001 The Education Center, Inc. • *Look 'n' Cook* • TEC604

118

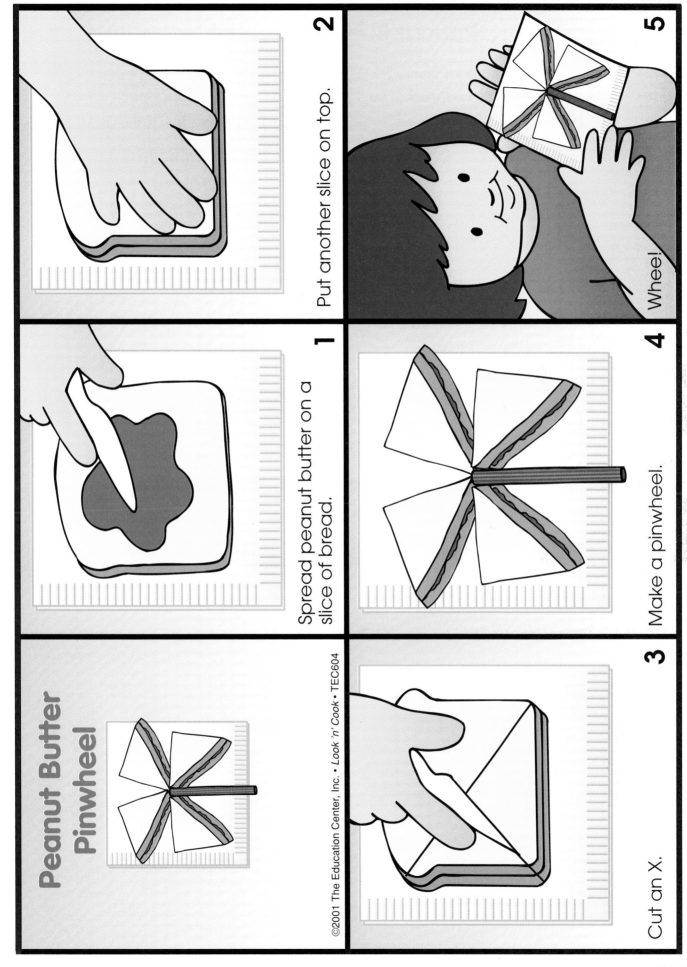

Peanut Butter Pinwheel

1 Spread peanut butter on a slice of bread.

2 Put another slice on top.

3 Cut an X.

4 Make a pinwheel.

5 Whee!

©2001 The Education Center, Inc. • *Look 'n' Cook* • TEC604

Peanut Butter Pinwheel

Pinwheels are a sign of spring! We are going to follow a simple recipe to make these windy-day snacks. To help us with this cooking project, please send in the item indicated below by _____. Thanks for making your child's learning fun and exciting!

___ loaf of sandwich bread

___ large package of red licorice sticks

___ jar of peanut butter

___ package of plastic knives

___ package of napkins

I made a **Peanut Butter Pinwheel** in school today!

My favorite part was _____.

It tasted _____.

This is what it looked like:

Chef's signature _____

An extra helping: On your next excursion to the library, check out *The Wind Blew* by Pat Hutchins. You will be blown away by the catchy verses and the mischievous wind!

Snail Biscuit

Race into springtime fun with this snail cooking idea. No slow moving here!

Ingredients for one:
1¹/₄ pieces of refrigerated biscuit dough
1 raisin (eye)
cinnamon sugar in a shaker

Utensils and supplies:
1 3" x 3" square of aluminum foil
    per child
permanent marker
knife
2 plastic plates
nonstick cookie sheet
oven
napkins

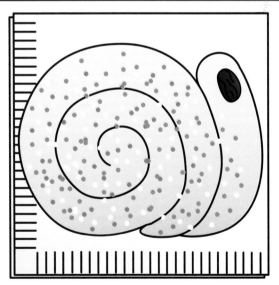

Teacher preparation:
• Personalize a class supply of aluminum foil squares.
• Cut enough refrigerated biscuits into fourths so that each child will have one piece; then place the pieces on a plate. Place a class supply of whole biscuits on a plate.
• Arrange the ingredients and supplies near the step-by-step direction cards.
• Bake the snail biscuits according to the package directions.

Snail Biscuit

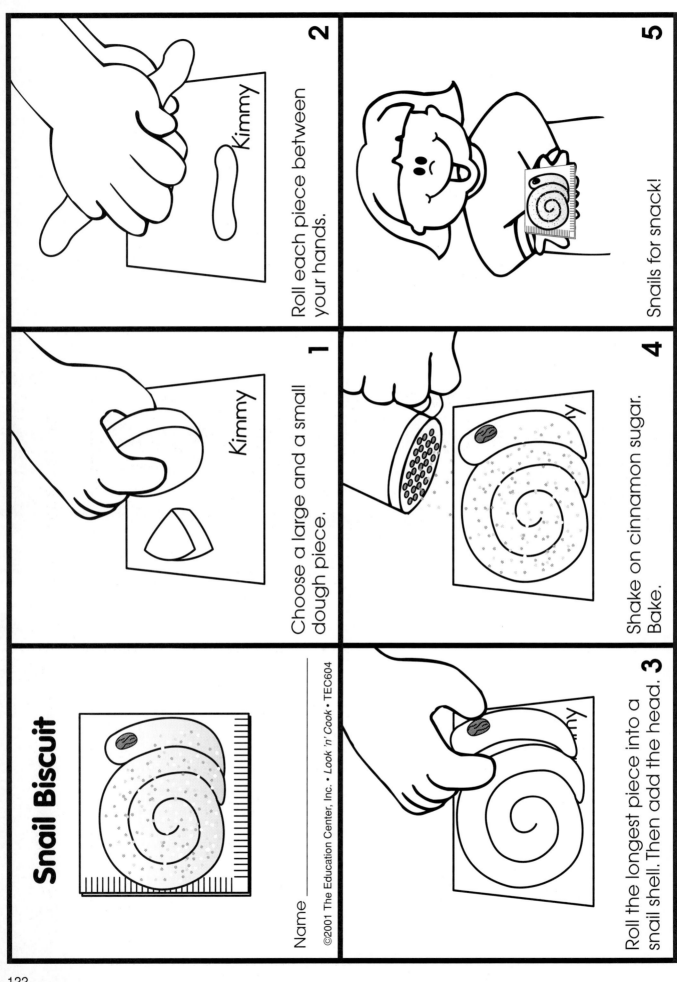

Name _____

©2001 The Education Center, Inc. • Look 'n' Cook • TEC604

1 Choose a large and a small dough piece.

2 Roll each piece between your hands.

3 Roll the longest piece into a snail shell. Then add the head.

4 Shake on cinnamon sugar. Bake.

5 Snails for snack!

Snail Biscuit

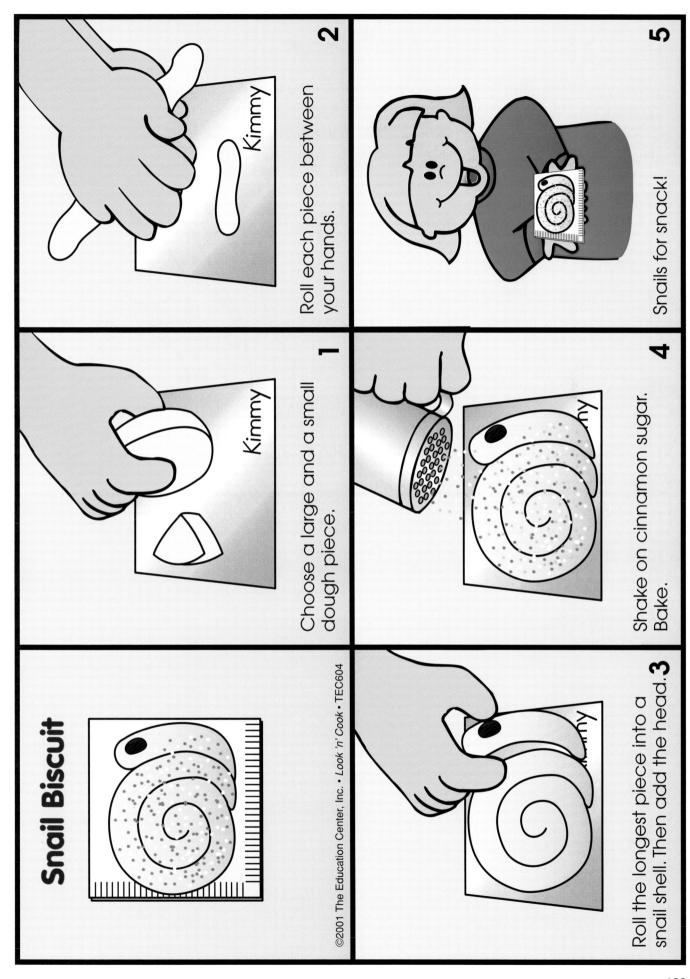

2 Roll each piece between your hands.

1 Choose a large and a small dough piece.

5 Snails for snack!

4 Shake on cinnamon sugar. Bake.

3 Roll the longest piece into a snail shell. Then add the head.

©2001 The Education Center, Inc. • *Look 'n' Cook* • TEC604

123

Snail Biscuit

On your next stroll outdoors, look for some snails moving along in the grass. In school, we're going to make snail biscuits. To help us with this cooking project, please send in the item indicated below by _____. Thanks for making your child's learning fun and exciting!

___ can of refrigerated biscuit dough

___ large box of raisins

___ shaker of cinnamon sugar

___ roll of aluminum foil

___ package of napkins

I made a **Snail Biscuit** in school today!

My favorite part was _____.

It tasted _____.

This is what it looked like:

Chef's signature _____

An extra helping: Check out the humorous tale *Snail Started It!* by Katja Reider.

Mud Pie

Splish, splash! What's more fun than making mud pies? Your little chefs will delight in creating this gooey mud recipe—raindrops included!

Ingredients for one:
$1/4$ c. milk
1 tbsp. chocolate instant pudding powder
1 miniature graham cracker pie crust
crushed chocolate sandwich cookies (soil)
blue candy sprinkles (raindrops)

Utensils and supplies:
1 resealable sandwich-sized plastic bag
$1/4$-cup measuring cup
tablespoon
safety scissors
1 plastic bowl
1 plastic spoon per child
napkins

Teacher preparation:
• Crush the cookies; then put them in the bowl.
• Arrange the ingredients and supplies near the step-by-step direction cards.

Mud Pie

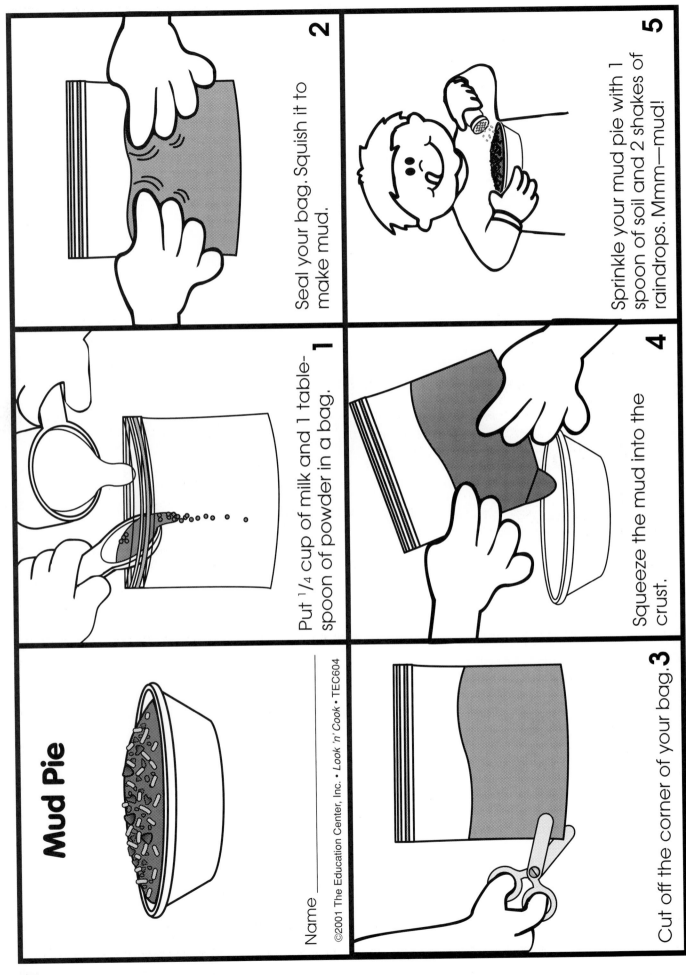

Name _____

1 Put ¼ cup of milk and 1 tablespoon of powder in a bag.

2 Seal your bag. Squish it to make mud.

3 Cut off the corner of your bag.

4 Squeeze the mud into the crust.

5 Sprinkle your mud pie with 1 spoon of soil and 2 shakes of raindrops. Mmm—mud!

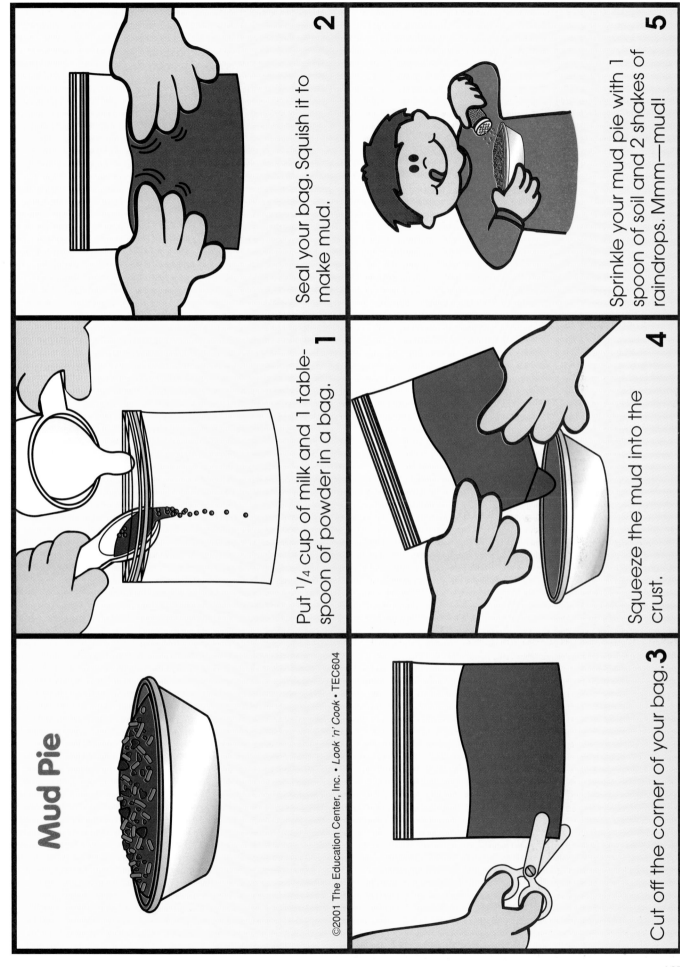

Mud Pie

1. Put 1/4 cup of milk and 1 tablespoon of powder in a bag.

2. Seal your bag. Squish it to make mud.

3. Cut off the corner of your bag!

4. Squeeze the mud into the crust.

5. Sprinkle your mud pie with 1 spoon of soil and 2 shakes of raindrops. Mmm—mud!

Mud Pie

We're going to celebrate rainy days by making some marvelous mud pies! To help us with this cooking project, please send in the item listed below by _____. Thanks for making your child's learning fun and exciting!

___ package of miniature graham cracker pie crusts

___ box of chocolate instant pudding mix

___ gallon of milk

___ package of chocolate sandwich cookies

___ container of blue candy sprinkles

___ box of resealable sandwich-sized plastic bags

___ package of plastic spoons

___ package of napkins

I made a **Mud Pie** in school today!

My favorite part was _____.

It tasted _____.

This is what it looked like:

Chef's signature _____

An extra helping: Read *Mud* by Mary Lyn Ray on a rainy day and then run and jump in some mud puddles!

Bunny Muffin

Bounce into warm weather with this healthy bunny recipe!

Ingredients for one:
1/2 plain English muffin (face)
2 rectangular slices of American cheese (ears)
6 chow mein noodles (whiskers)
2 circular carrot slices (eyes)
1 triangular cucumber slice (nose)
cream cheese

Utensils and supplies:
3 paper plates
knife
toaster
1 plastic knife per child
napkins

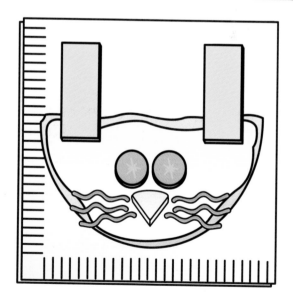

Teacher preparation:
• Split the English muffins; then cut each in half.
• Allow the cream cheese to soften.
• Cut the carrots into discs and put them on a plate.
• Cut the cheese into rectangular pieces and put them on a plate.
• Cut the cucumber into triangular pieces and put them on a plate.
• Arrange the ingredients and supplies near the step-by-step direction cards.
• Help each child toast her muffin as needed.

Bunny Muffin

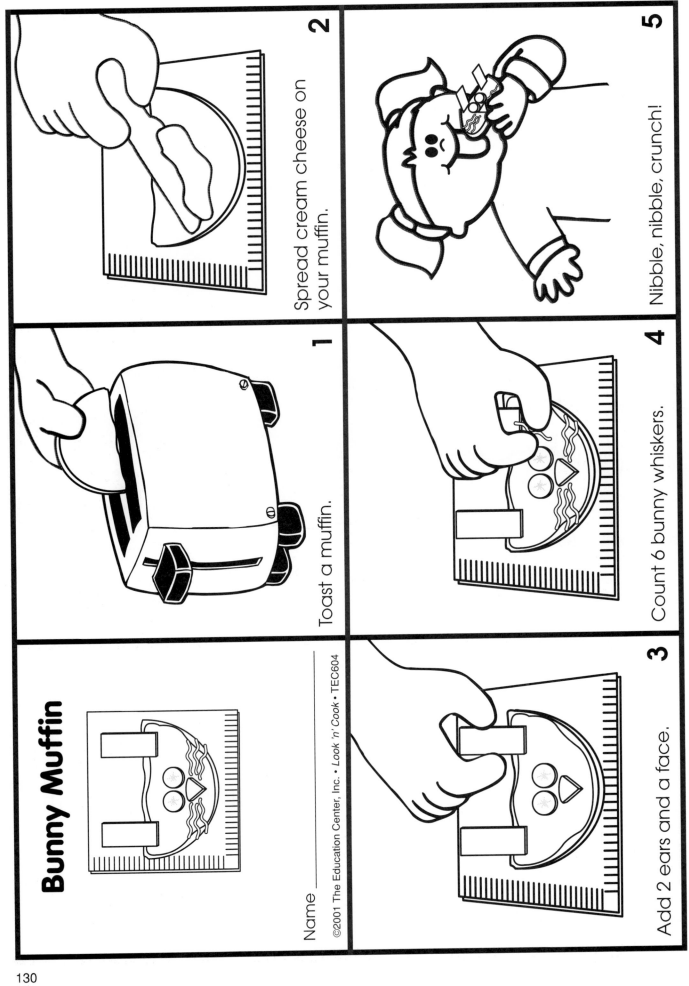

Name _____

©2001 The Education Center, Inc. • Look 'n' Cook • TEC604

1 Toast a muffin.

2 Spread cream cheese on your muffin.

3 Add 2 ears and a face.

4 Count 6 bunny whiskers.

5 Nibble, nibble, crunch!

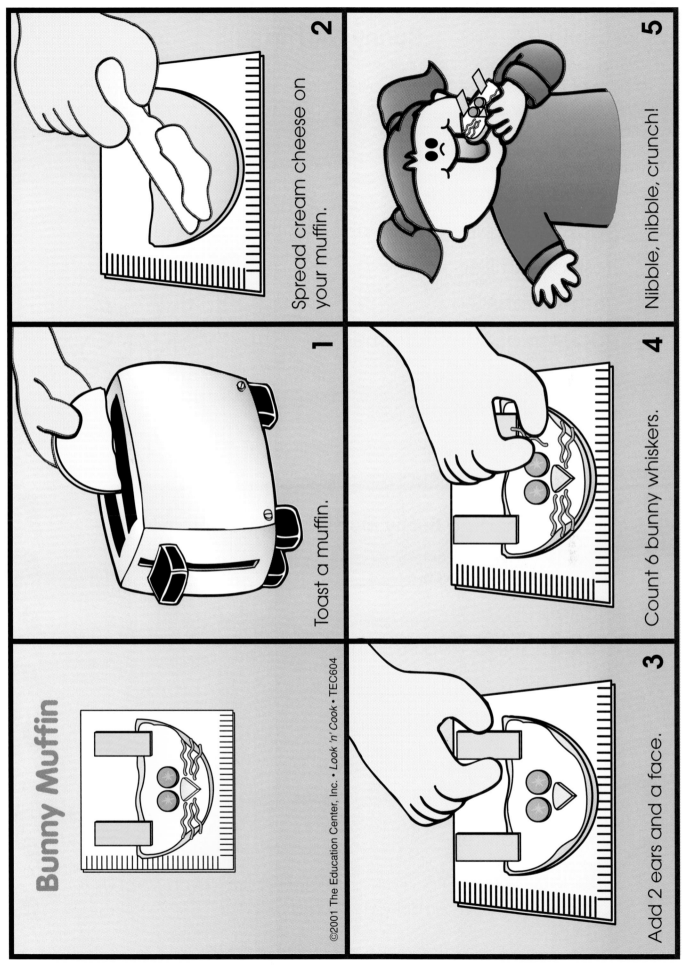

Bunny Muffin

©2001 The Education Center, Inc. • *Look 'n' Cook* • TEC604

1

Toast a muffin.

2

Spread cream cheese on your muffin.

3

Add 2 ears and a face.

4

Count 6 bunny whiskers.

5

Nibble, nibble, crunch!

Bunny Muffin

After learning about bunnies, we're going to create a nutritious snack to nibble! To help us with this cooking project, please send in the item indicated below by _____. Thanks for making your child's learning fun and exciting!

___ bag of English muffins

___ package of plain cream cheese

___ fresh cucumber

___ fresh carrots

___ package of American cheese

___ container of chow mein noodles

___ package of plastic knives

___ package of napkins

I made a **Bunny Muffin** in school today!

My favorite part was _____.

It tasted _____.

This is what it looked like:

Chef's signature _____

An extra helping: For a delightful spring story, read *Rabbits & Raindrops* by Jim Arnosky. Hop, hop!

Quick Chick

This simple recipe will have your little ones chirping with cooking enthusiasm!

Ingredients for one:
1 small round cracker (head)
1 large round cracker (body)
cream cheese
4 triangular carrot slices (beak, wing, feet)
1 raisin (eye)

Utensils and supplies:
knife
1 plastic bowl
1 plastic knife per child
yellow food coloring
napkins

Teacher preparation:
- Allow the cream cheese to soften slightly. Tint the cream cheese with yellow food coloring.
- Cut a class supply of triangular carrot slices; then place them in a bowl.
- Arrange the ingredients and supplies near the step-by-step direction cards.

Quick Chick

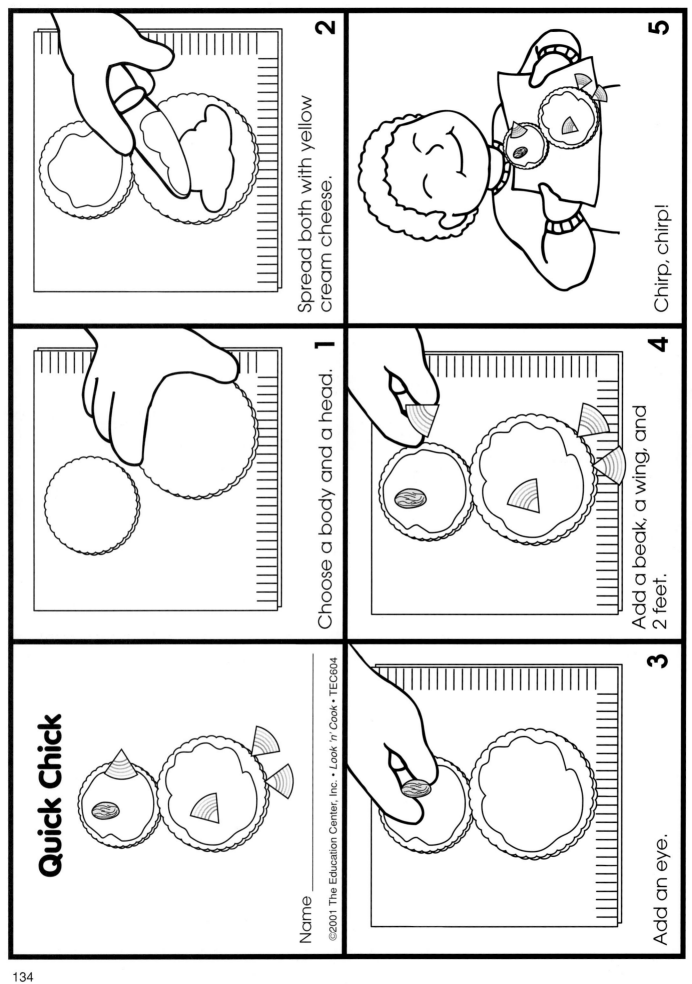

Name _____

1 Choose a body and a head.

2 Spread both with yellow cream cheese.

3 Add an eye.

4 Add a beak, a wing, and 2 feet.

5 Chirp, chirp!

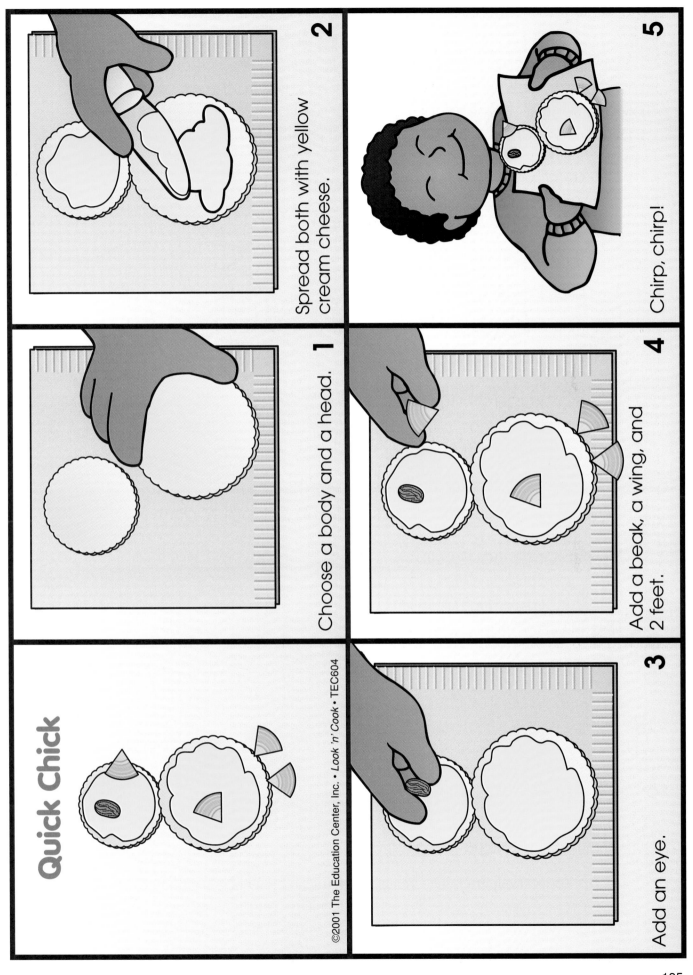

Quick Chick

©2001 The Education Center, Inc. • *Look 'n' Cook* • TEC604

1 Choose a body and a head.

2 Spread both with yellow cream cheese.

3 Add an eye.

4 Add a beak, a wing, and 2 feet.

5 Chirp, chirp!

Quick Chick

Spring is hatching everywhere, so in school we are going to make some yellow chick snacks. To help us with this cooking project, please send in the item indicated below by _____. Thanks for making your child's learning fun and exciting!

___ box of small round crackers

___ box of large round crackers

___ tub of cream cheese

___ package of food coloring

___ bag of carrots

___ large box of raisins

___ package of napkins

___ package of plastic knives

©2001 The Education Center, Inc. • *Look 'n' Cook* • TEC604

I made a **Quick Chick** in school today!

My favorite part was _____.

It tasted _____.

This is what it looked like:

Chef's signature _____

An extra helping: On your next trip to the library, check out *Dora's Eggs* by Julie Sykes. It's an interesting story about a hen who likes her eggs, but likes something else even more!

©2001 The Education Center, Inc. • *Look 'n' Cook* • TEC604

Metamorphosnack

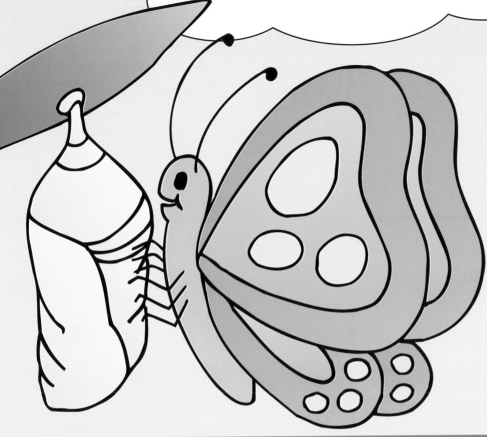

Planning on studying butterflies? This healthy snack simulates a butterfly emerging from its cocoon. Flutter, butterflies!

Ingredients for one:
1 slice of sandwich bread
1 cucumber spear
cream cheese

Utensils and supplies:
plastic bowl
butterfly-shaped cookie cutter
1 plastic knife per child
napkins

Teacher preparation:
- Peel the cucumbers and then cut them into spears. Put them in a bowl.
- Allow the cream cheese to soften slightly.
- Arrange the ingredients and supplies near the step-by-step direction cards.

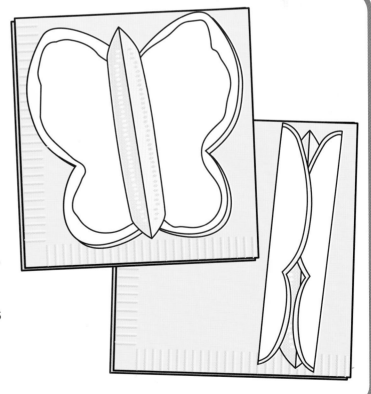

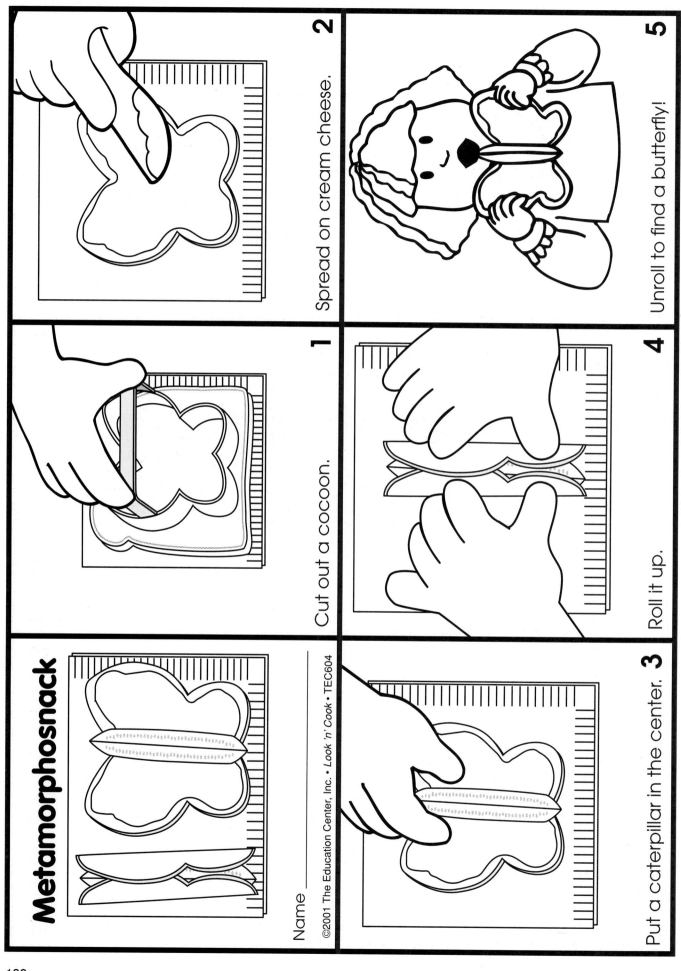

Metamorphosnack

Name _____

©2001 The Education Center, Inc. • *Look 'n' Cook* • TEC604

1. Cut out a cocoon.

2. Spread on cream cheese.

3. Put a caterpillar in the center!

4. Roll it up.

5. Unroll to find a butterfly!

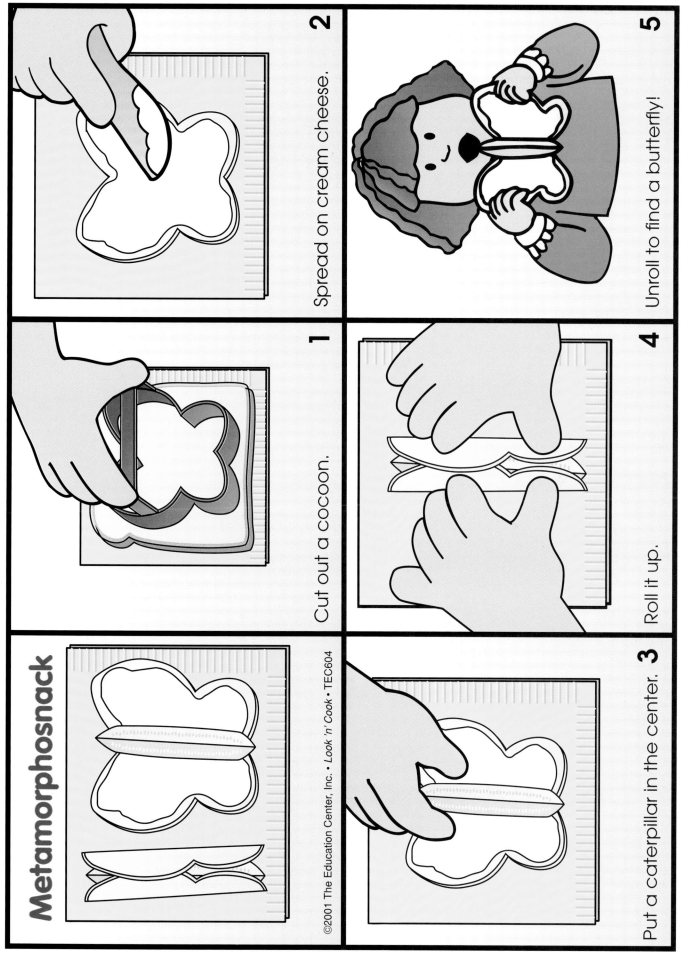

Metamorphosnack

2 Spread on cream cheese.

5 Unroll to find a butterfly!

1 Cut out a cocoon.

4 Roll it up.

3 Put a caterpillar in the center!

©2001 The Education Center, Inc. • *Look 'n' Cook* • TEC604

Metamorphosnack

We're going to make an edible caterpillar and then change it into a butterfly! To help us with this cooking project, please send in the item indicated below by _____. Thanks for making your child's learning fun and exciting!

___ loaf of sandwich bread

___ cucumbers

___ tub of cream cheese

___ package of plastic knives

___ package of napkins

I made a **Metamorphosnack** in school today!

My favorite part was _____.

It tasted _____.

This is what it looked like:

Chef's signature _____

An extra helping: Read *The Caterpillow Fight* by Sam McBratney and have a good chuckle!

Peanut Butter Bug

These yummy little critters will get your youngsters buggy about insects!

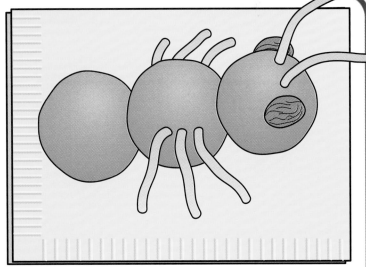

Ingredients for one:
$1/4$ c. peanut butter mix (see
   instructions below)
8 chow mein noodles (antennae
   and legs)
2 raisins (eyes)

Utensils and supplies:
1 plastic bowl
1 3" x 3" square of waxed paper
   per child
napkins

Teacher preparation:
- To make enough peanut butter mix
  for eight students, combine two cups of powdered milk, $1 1/2$
  cups of peanut butter, and one-half cup of honey in a bowl.
  Divide the mixture into $1/4$-cup portions.
- Arrange the ingredients and supplies near the step-by-step
  direction cards.

Peanut Butter Bug

Name _____

2 Make a body.

1 Divide the dough into 3 pieces. Roll each piece into a ball.

3 Add two eyes.

4 Add 6 legs. Add 2 antennae.

5 Eat it before it crawls away!

Peanut Butter Bug

2 Make a body.

1 Divide the dough into 3 pieces. Roll each piece into a ball.

3 Add two eyes.

4 Add 6 legs. Add 2 antennae.

5 Eat it before it crawls away!

©2001 The Education Center, Inc. • *Look 'n' Cook* • TEC604

Peanut Butter Bug

Insects are not always creepy and crawly. To prove it, we are going to make a batch of cute and tasty bugs! To help us with this cooking project, please send in the item indicated below by _____. Thanks for making your child's learning fun and exciting!

___ roll of waxed paper

___ box of powdered milk

___ jar of peanut butter

___ jar of honey

___ container of chow mein noodles

___ large box of raisins

___ package of napkins

I made a **Peanut Butter Bug** in school today!

My favorite part was _____.

It tasted _____.

This is what it looked like:

Chef's signature _____

An extra helping: Next time you visit your local library, check out *Step by Step* by Diane Wolkstein for an interesting story about ants.

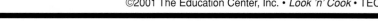

May Flower

No April showers necessary—these sweet May flowers will bloom in any weather!

Ingredients for one:
1 vanilla wafer
peanut butter
5 red or yellow apple slices
one 3" piece of celery

Utensils and supplies:
knife
1 large plastic bowl
1 plastic plate
1 plastic knife per child
napkins

Teacher preparation:
- Cut a class supply of apple slices; then, if desired, toss them in diluted lemon juice or lemon-lime soda to prevent browning. Place them in the bowl.
- Cut a class supply of three-inch celery pieces; then put them on the plate.
- Arrange the ingredients and supplies near the step-by-step direction cards.

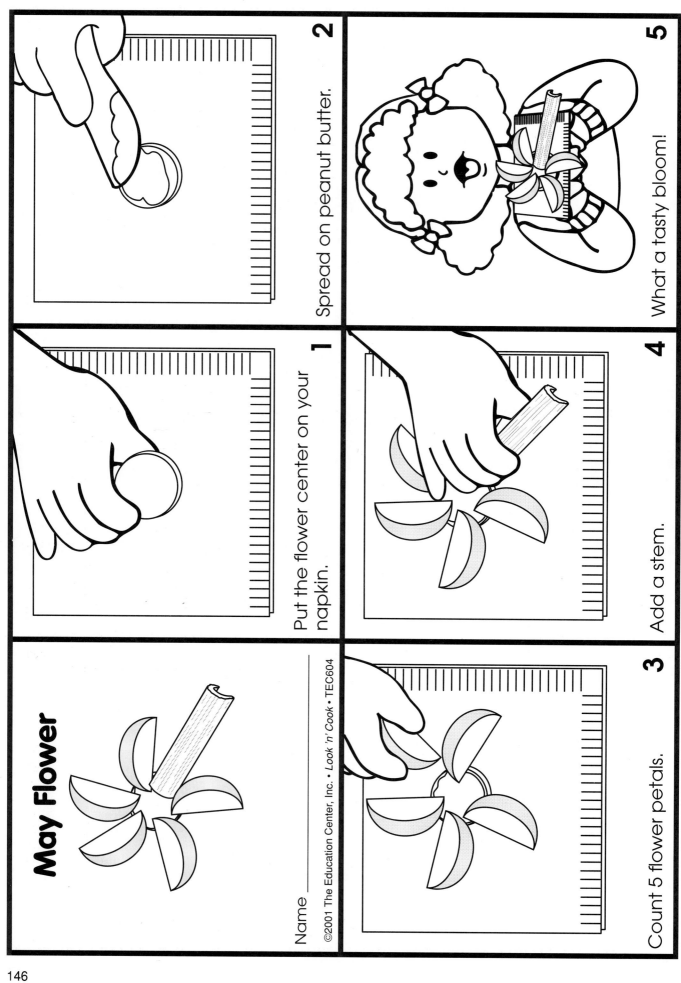

May Flower

Name _____

©2001 The Education Center, Inc. • Look 'n' Cook • TEC604

1 Put the flower center on your napkin.

2 Spread on peanut butter.

3 Count 5 flower petals.

4 Add a stem.

5 What a tasty bloom!

May Flower

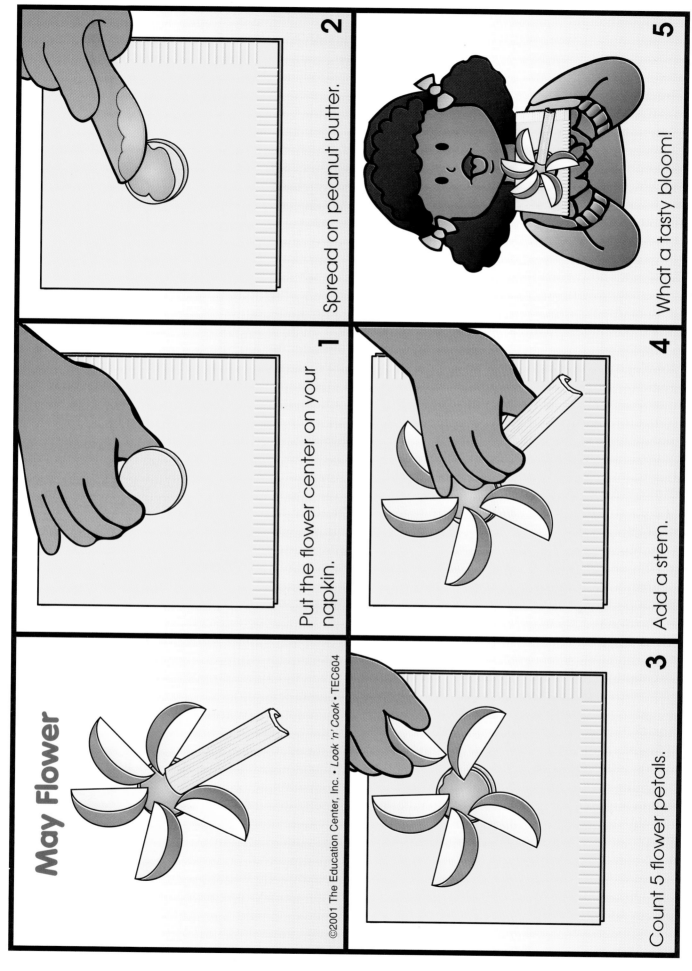

1 Put the flower center on your napkin.

2 Spread on peanut butter.

3 Count 5 flower petals.

4 Add a stem.

5 What a tasty bloom!

©2001 The Education Center, Inc. • *Look 'n' Cook* • TEC604

May Flower

Snacktime will bloom with good taste when we prepare these sweet May flowers! To help us with this cooking project, please send in the item indicated below by _____. Thanks for making your child's learning fun and exciting!

___ bag of red or yellow apples

___ box of vanilla wafers

___ jar of peanut butter

___ bunch of fresh celery

___ package of plastic knives

___ package of napkins

I made a **May Flower** in school today!

My favorite part was _____.

It tasted _____.

This is what it looked like:

Chef's signature _____

An extra helping: Have bunches of fun reading *Counting Wildflowers* by Bruce McMillan. Stop by the library today!

Fruity Tart

After a long winter, summer fruits are a welcome sight. Have your youngsters make these summery-sweet tarts!

Ingredients for one:
1 individual shortcake
1 peach slice (canned or fresh)
1 spoonful of strawberry slices
5 blueberries
whipped topping

Utensils and supplies:
3 plastic bowls
1 plastic spoon per child
napkins

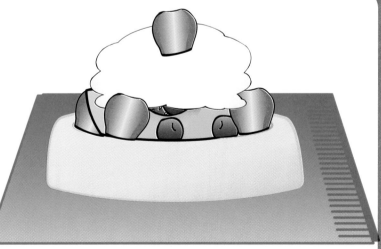

Teacher preparation:
- Put each kind of fruit in a separate bowl.
- Arrange the ingredients and supplies near the step-by-step direction cards.

Fruity Tart

©2001 The Education Center, Inc. • Look 'n' Cook • TEC604

Name _____

1 Put a shortcake on your napkin.

2 Put 1 peach slice in the shortcake.

3 Add 1 spoonful of strawberries.

4 Count 5 blueberries.

5 Add whipped topping and a strawberry. Yum!

Fruity Tart

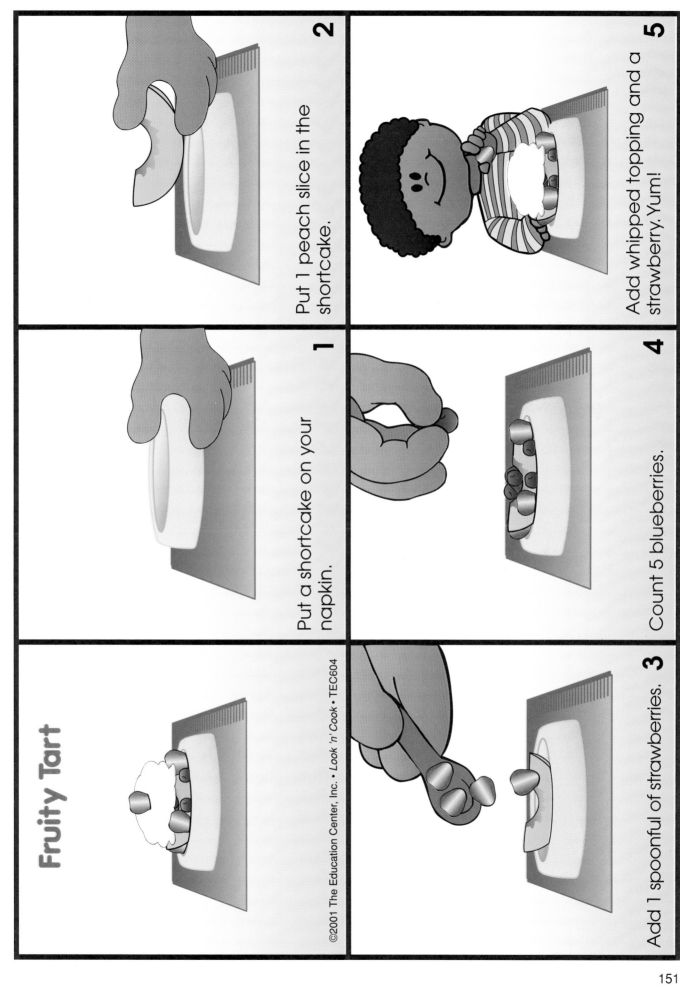

2
Put 1 peach slice in the shortcake.

5
Add whipped topping and a strawberry. Yum!

1
Put a shortcake on your napkin.

4
Count 5 blueberries.

3
Add 1 spoonful of strawberries.

©2001 The Education Center, Inc. • *Look 'n' Cook* • TEC604

151

Fruity Tart

Summer's almost here! We're going to follow a simple recipe to make a refreshing fruity snack for a warm day. To help us with this cooking project, please send in the item indicated below by _____. Thanks for making your child's learning fun and exciting!

___ package of individual shortcakes

___ fresh peaches or a large can of sliced peaches

___ container of fresh strawberries or a bag of frozen strawberries

___ container of fresh blueberries or a bag of frozen blueberries

___ container of whipped topping

___ package of plastic spoons

___ package of napkins

I made a **Fruity Tart** in school today!

My favorite part was _____.

It tasted _____.

This is what it looked like:

Chef's signature _____

An extra helping: Visit your local library and check out *The First Strawberries: A Cherokee Story* retold by Joseph Bruchac.

Graduate Cone

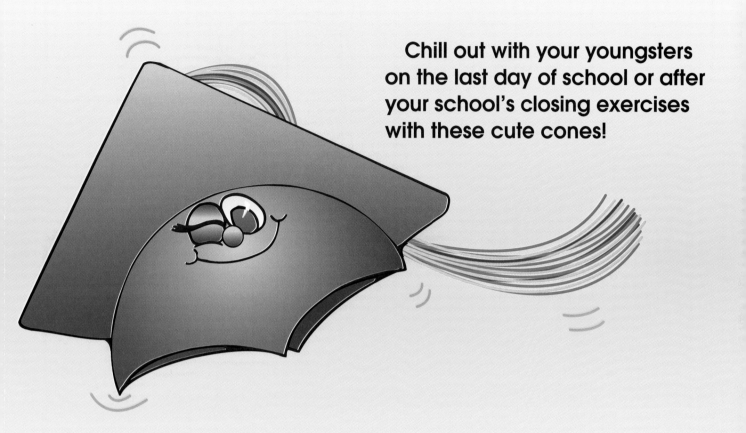

Chill out with your youngsters on the last day of school or after your school's closing exercises with these cute cones!

Ingredients for one:
1 flat-bottomed ice-cream cone (body)
1 scoop of ice cream (face)
8 chocolate chips (eyes, nose, and mouth)
1 chocolate graham cracker square (hat)
chocolate frosting
one 2" length of black string licorice (tassel)

Utensils and supplies:
2 plastic bowls
ice-cream scoop
1 plastic knife per child
1 small paper plate per child
napkins

Teacher preparation:
- Break apart enough graham cracker sheets into squares for each child to have one; then place the squares in a bowl.
- Cut the licorice into two-inch lengths and place them in a bowl.
- Allow the ice cream to soften slightly.
- Arrange the ingredients and supplies near the step-by-step direction cards.

Graduate Cone

2 Make a happy face.

5 Happy graduation!

1 Put 1 scoop of ice cream into your cone.

4 Add a tassel.

3 Frost 1 graham cracker square.

Name _____

Graduate Cone

2 Make a happy face.

5 Happy graduation!

1 Put 1 scoop of ice cream into your cone.

4 Add a tassel.

3 Frost 1 graham cracker square.

©2001 The Education Center, Inc. • *Look 'n' Cook* • TEC604

Graduate Cone

The school year is coming to a close. We are going to follow simple directions to make graduate cone snacks. To help with this cooking project, please send in the item indicated below by _____. Thanks for making your child's learning fun and exciting!

___ box of flat-bottomed ice-cream cones

___ container of _____ ice cream

___ bag of chocolate chips

___ box of chocolate graham crackers

___ can of chocolate frosting

___ package of black string licorice

___ package of plastic knives

___ package of small paper plates

___ package of napkins

I made a **Graduate Cone** in school today!

My favorite part was _____.

It tasted _____.

This is what it looked like:

Chef's signature _____

An extra helping: Read the rhythmic story *Oh, the Places You'll Go!* by Dr. Seuss. How inspiring!

Sunrise Surprise

Start off the morning by helping your little ones make these sunshiny treats!

Ingredients for one:
1 piece of refrigerated biscuit dough
1 cube of cheddar cheese
melted butter or margarine

Utensils and supplies:
one 5" square of aluminum foil per child
permanent marker
plastic bowl
1 plastic fork per child
small basting brush
nonstick cookie sheet
oven
1 paper plate per child
napkins

Teacher preparation:
- Personalize a foil square for each child.
- Melt the butter or margarine. Let it cool a little; then pour it into the bowl.
- Arrange the ingredients and supplies near the step-by-step direction cards.
- Bake the biscuits according to the package directions.

Sunrise Surprise

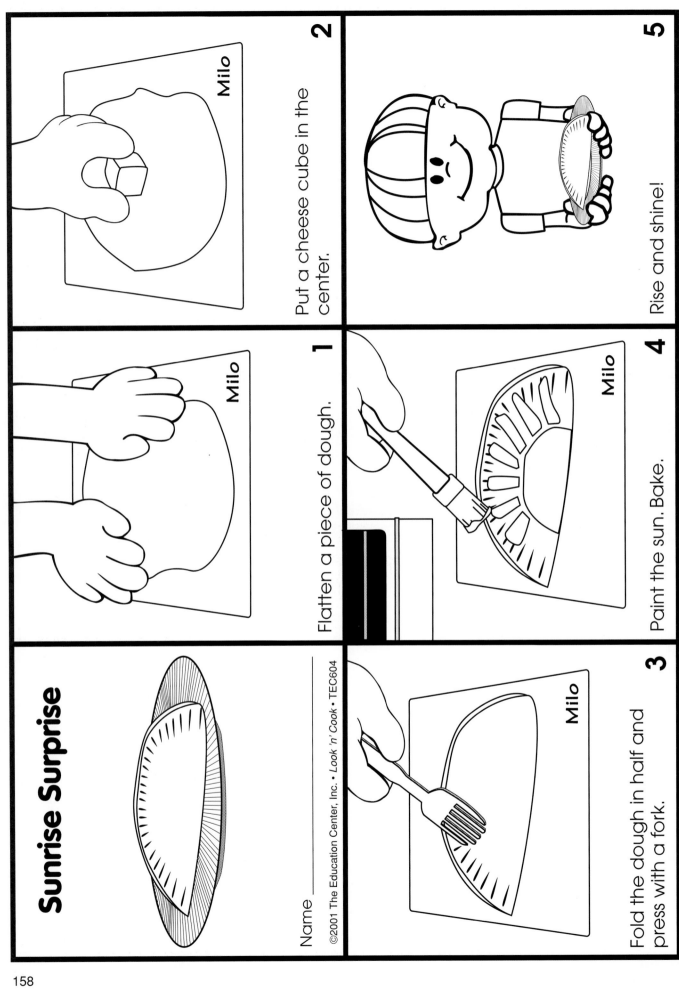

Name _____

1 Milo

Flatten a piece of dough.

2 Milo

Put a cheese cube in the center.

3 Milo

Fold the dough in half and press with a fork.

4 Milo

Paint the sun. Bake.

5

Rise and shine!

158

Sunrise Surprise

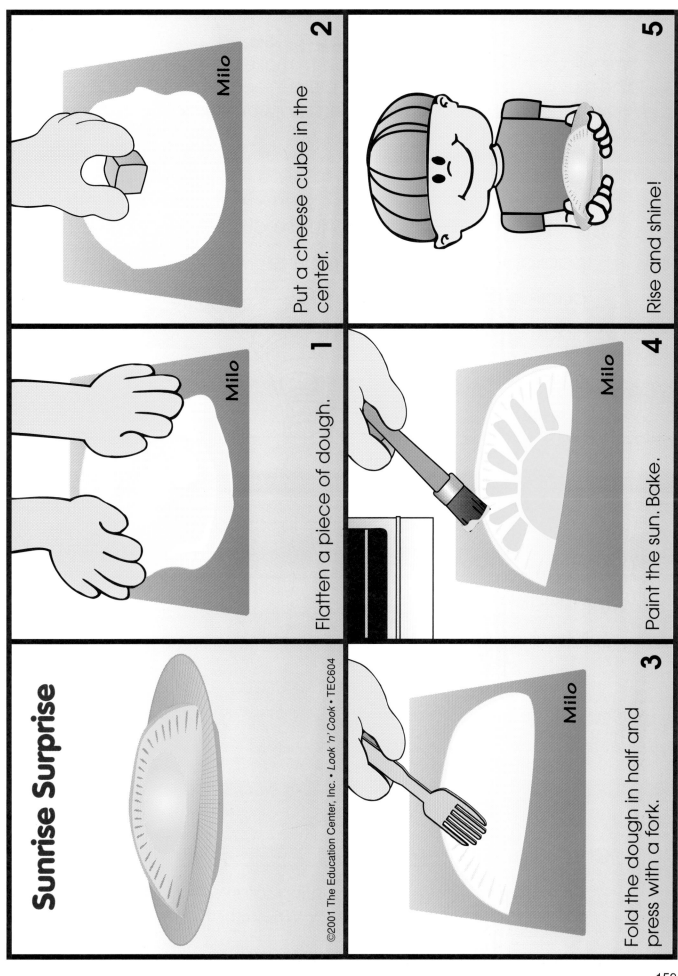

2 Put a cheese cube in the center.

Milo

5 Rise and shine!

1 Flatten a piece of dough.

Milo

4 Paint the sun. Bake.

Milo

©2001 The Education Center, Inc. • Look 'n' Cook • TEC604

3 Fold the dough in half and press with a fork.

Milo

159

Sunrise Surprise

We will be following a simple recipe to make a sunny morning treat! To help us with this cooking project, please send in the item indicated below by _____. Thanks for making your child's learning fun and exciting!

___ can of refrigerated biscuits

___ prepackaged cheddar cheese cubes

___ package of butter or margarine

___ package of plastic forks

___ package of paper plates

___ package of napkins

I made a **Sunrise Surprise** in school today!

My favorite part was _____.

It tasted _____.

This is what it looked like:

Chef's signature _____

An extra helping: Go on a counting safari with the book *Following the Sun* by Jenny Stow. Whew, that sun's bright!

Sweet Sparkler

Spark your little firecrackers' interest in baking with these patriotic snacks!

Ingredients for one:
refrigerated sugar cookie dough
vanilla frosting
red, white, and blue candy sprinkles

Utensils and supplies:
1 plastic plate
one 6" x 4" rectangle of aluminum foil per child
permanent marker
nonstick cookie sheet
oven
1 plastic knife per child
napkins

Teacher preparation:
• Personalize a class supply of aluminum foil rectangles.
• Freeze the roll of cookie dough for approximately 15 minutes; then cut it into half-inch slices to make a class supply.
• Pour the candy sprinkles on a plate.
• Arrange the ingredients and supplies near the step-by-step direction cards.
• Bake the cookies according to the package directions.

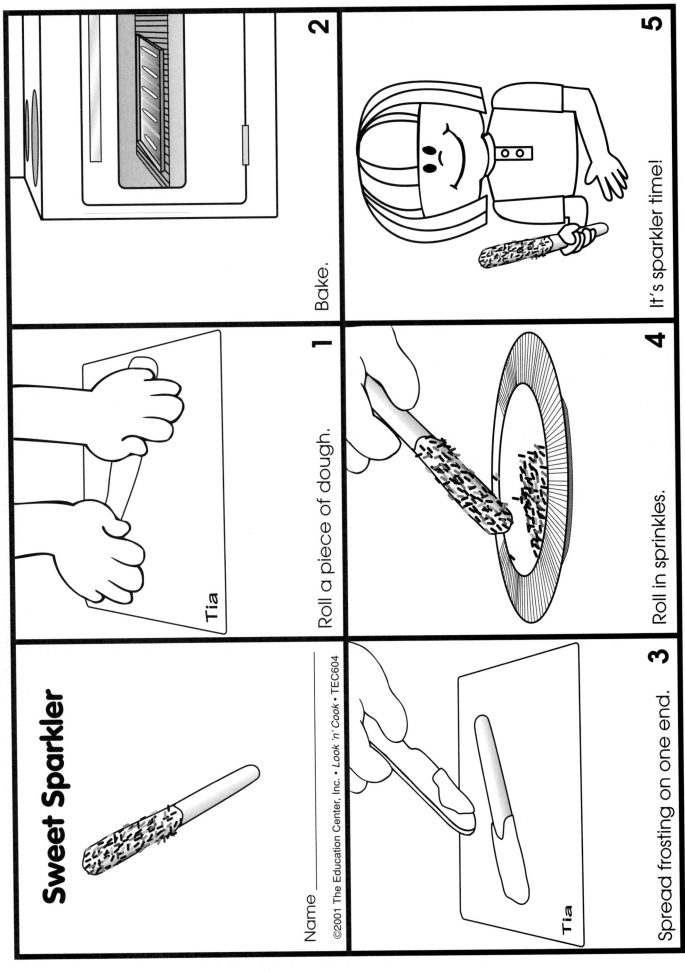

Sweet Sparkler

Name _____

©2001 The Education Center, Inc. • Look 'n' Cook • TEC604

1 Roll a piece of dough.

2 Bake.

3 Spread frosting on one end.

4 Roll in sprinkles.

5 It's sparkler time!

Sweet Sparkler

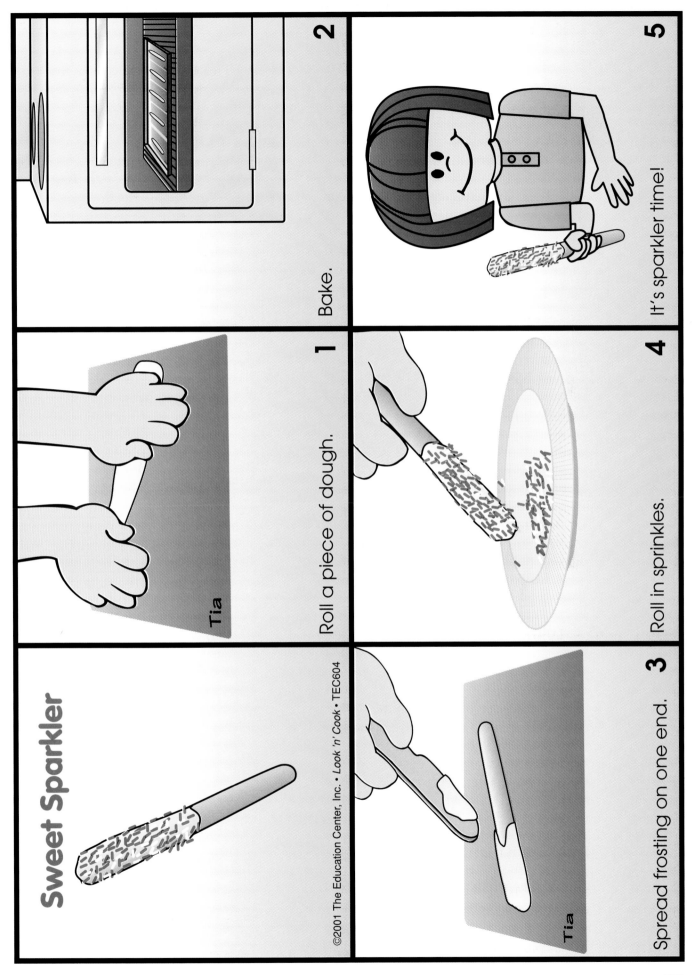

2

Bake.

1

Tia

Roll a piece of dough.

©2001 The Education Center, Inc. • *Look 'n' Cook* • TEC604

5

It's sparkler time!

4

Roll in sprinkles.

3

Tia

Spread frosting on one end.

63

Sweet Sparkler

We are going to make some yummy red, white, and blue sparklers to celebrate our nation's birthday! To help us with this cooking project, please send in the item indicated below by _____. Thanks for making your child's learning fun and exciting!

___ roll of refrigerated sugar cookie dough

___ can of vanilla frosting

___ container of red, white, and blue
    candy sprinkles

___ roll of aluminum foil

___ package of plastic knives

___ package of napkins

I made a **Sweet Sparkler** in school today!

My favorite part was _____.

It tasted _____.

This is what it looked like:

Chef's signature _____

An extra helping: On your next trip to the library, check out *Happy Birthday, America!* by Marsha Wilson Chall. Hooray—it's the Fourth of July!

American Flag

Salute the stars and stripes with these cool snacktime treats!

Ingredients for one:
$1/2$" slice of pound cake
6 blueberries
red cake decorating gel
one 4" length of Twizzlers® candy

Utensils and supplies:
knife
1 plastic plate
1 paper plate per child
napkins

Teacher preparation:
- Cut the pound cake into $1/2$-inch-thick slices and place on the plate.
- Arrange the ingredients and supplies near the step-by-step direction cards.

American Flag

Name _____

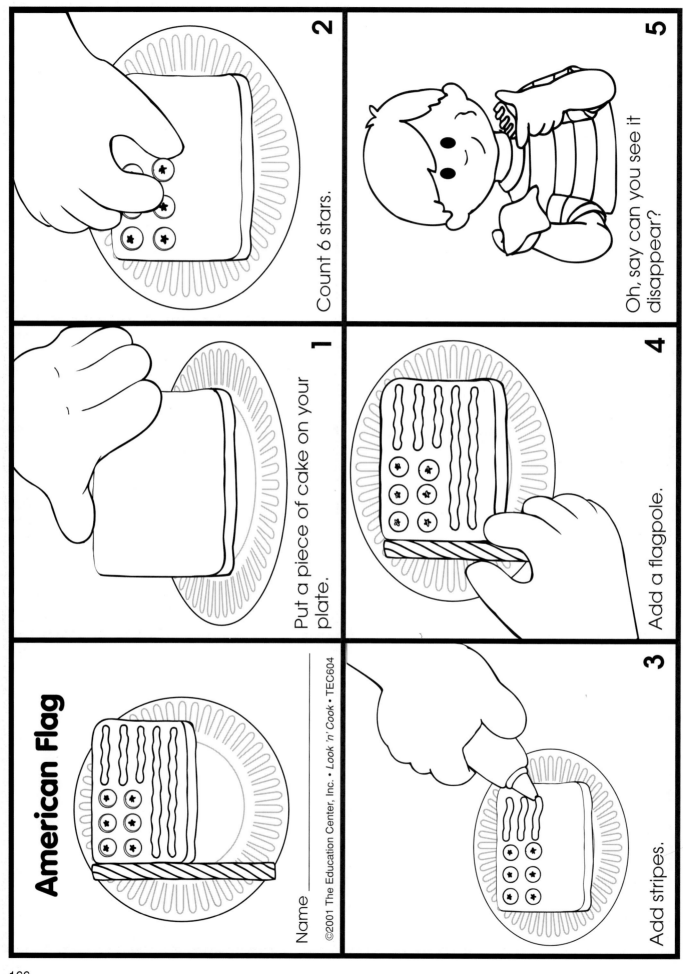

2 Count 6 stars.

5 Oh, say can you see it disappear?

1 Put a piece of cake on your plate.

4 Add a flagpole.

3 Add stripes.

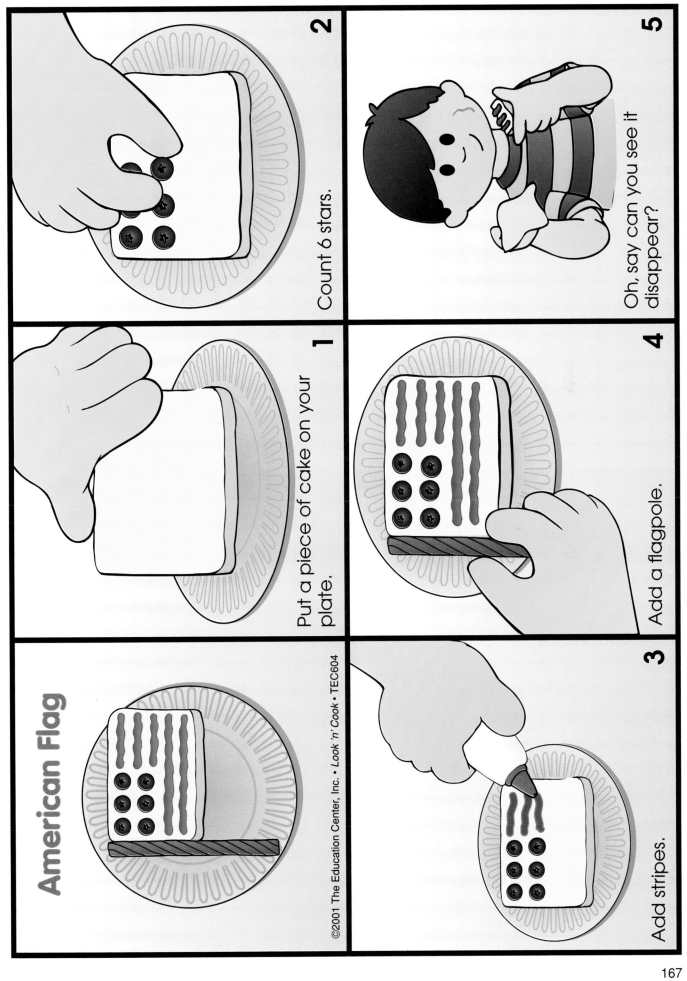

American Flag

2 Count 6 stars.

1 Put a piece of cake on your plate.

5 Oh, say can you see it disappear?

4 Add a flagpole.

3 Add stripes.

©2001 The Education Center, Inc. • *Look 'n' Cook* • TEC604

American Flag

We're going to catch some Fourth of July spirit when we make these fantastic flag treats! To help us with this cooking project, please send in the item indicated below by _____. Thanks for making your child's learning fun and exciting!

___ prepackaged loaf of pound cake

___ container of fresh or frozen blueberries

___ tube of red cake decorating gel

___ bag of Twizzlers® candy

___ package of paper plates

___ package of plastic spoons

___ package of napkins

I made an **American Flag** in school today!

My favorite part was _____.

It tasted _____.

This is what it looked like:

Chef's signature _____

An extra helping: Enjoy *America the Beautiful* by Katharine Lee Bates. This book tells all about one of our favorite patriotic songs!

Patriotic Parfait

Your students are sure to have a blast making this tricolored treat!

Ingredients for one:
vanilla yogurt
red, white, and blue candy sprinkles
1 JET-PUFFED® StarMallows® marshmallow

Utensils and supplies:
3 plastic bowls
red food coloring
blue food coloring
one 8-oz. clear plastic cup per child
1 plastic spoon per child
napkins

Teacher preparation:
- Divide the yogurt into each of three separate bowls.
- Use food coloring to tint one bowl of yogurt red and another blue. Leave one bowl of yogurt white.
- Arrange the ingredients and supplies near the step-by-step direction cards.

Patriotic Parfait

Name _____

2 Add white yogurt.

1 Add red yogurt.

3 Add blue yogurt.

4 Top with sprinkles and a marshmallow.

5 Happy birthday, America!

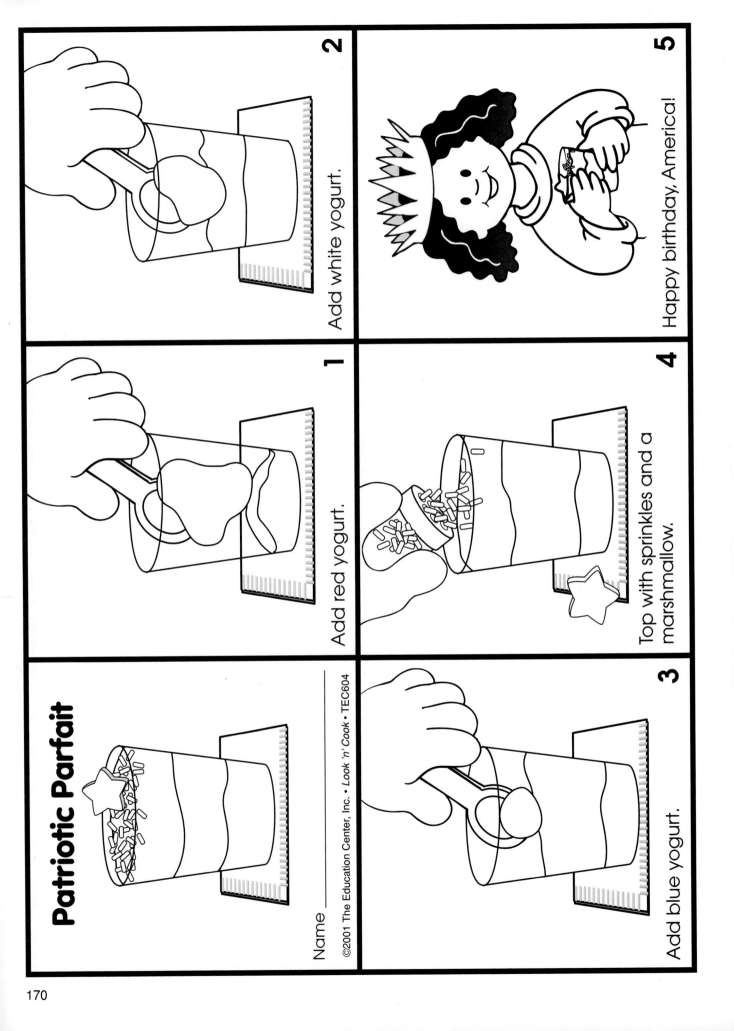

Patriotic Parfait

2

Add white yogurt.

1

Add red yogurt.

5

Happy birthday, America!

4

Top with sprinkles and a marshmallow.

3

Add blue yogurt.

Patriotic Parfait

Fireworks and stars in the sky—it's time to show our patriotism! In school, we're going to enjoy a special snack. To help us with this cooking project, please send in the item indicated below by _____. Thanks for making your child's learning fun and exciting!

___ large container of vanilla yogurt

___ red, white, and blue candy sprinkles

___ large bag of JET-PUFFED® StarMallows® marshmallows

___ package of food coloring

___ package of 8-oz. clear plastic cups

___ package of plastic spoons

___ package of napkins

I made a **Patriotic Parfait** in school today!

My favorite part was _____.

It tasted _____.

This is what it looked like:

Chef's signature _____

An extra helping: Sing along with the delightful book *This Land Is Your Land* by Woody Guthrie!

Summer Sunflower

These sunny-day snacks will brighten up your snacktime!

Ingredients for one:
1 round butter cracker
cream cheese
10 Bugles® corn snacks
sunflower seeds, shelled

Utensils and supplies:
yellow food coloring
1 plastic knife per child
napkins

Teacher preparation:
* Allow the cream cheese to soften slightly; then tint it with yellow food coloring.
* Arrange the ingredients and supplies near the step-by-step direction cards.

2

Spread cream cheese.

5

Delightful!

1

Put a round cracker on your napkin.

4

Add sunflower seeds.

Summer Sunflower

Name: _____

©2001 The Education Center, Inc. • *Look 'n' Cook* • TEC604

3

Count 10 petals.

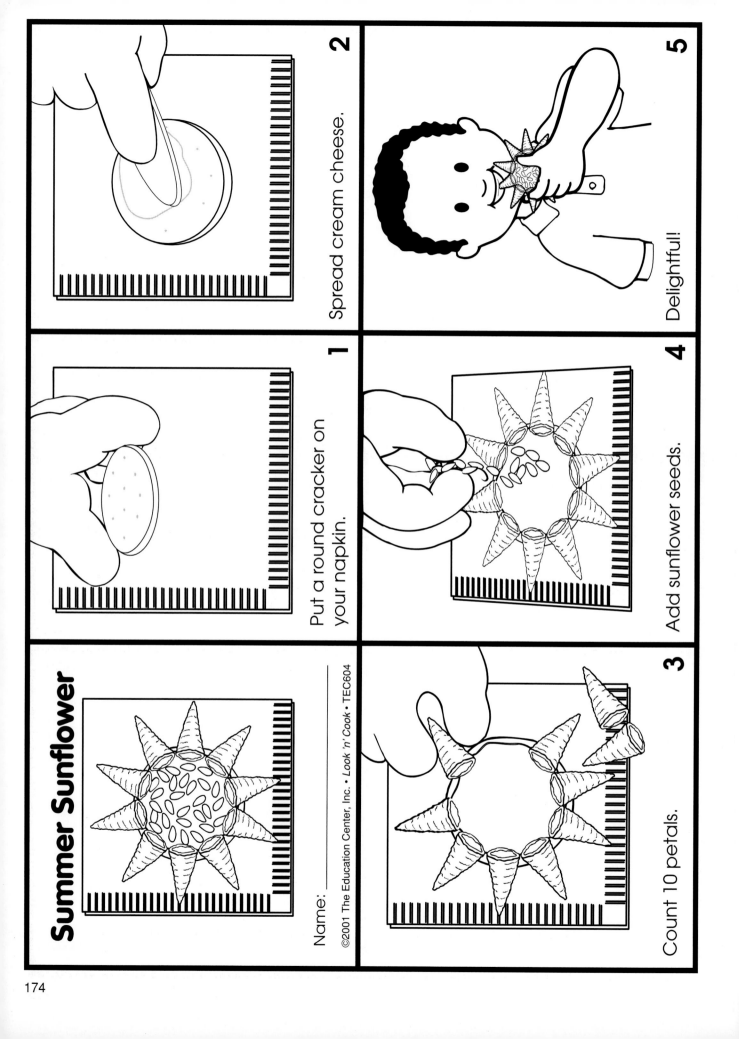

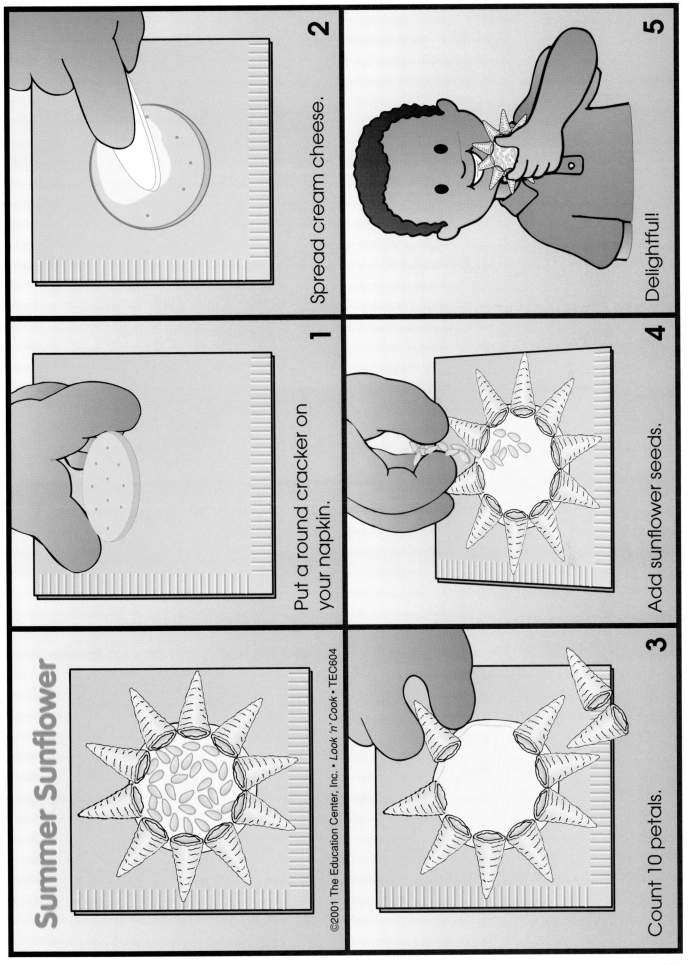

Summer Sunflower

2 Spread cream cheese.

1 Put a round cracker on your napkin.

5 Delightfull!

4 Add sunflower seeds.

3 Count 10 petals.

Summer Sunflower

Your child will bloom with pride after making this sunny snack! To help us with this cooking project, please send in the item indicated below by _____. Thanks for making your child's learning fun and exciting!

___ box of round butter crackers (such as Ritz® crackers)

___ tub of soft cream cheese

___ large bag of Bugles® corn snacks

___ large bag of sunflower seeds, shelled

___ package of food coloring

___ package of plastic knives

___ package of napkins

I made a **Summer Sunflower** in school today!

My favorite part was _____.

It tasted _____.

This is what it looked like:

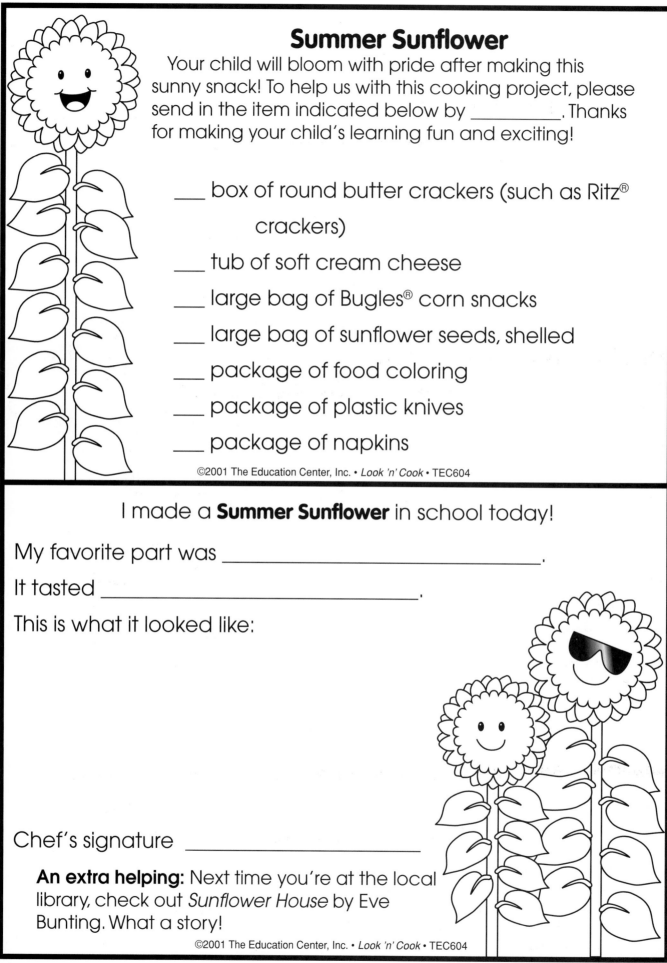

Chef's signature _____

An extra helping: Next time you're at the local library, check out *Sunflower House* by Eve Bunting. What a story!

Tropical Fish

Youngsters will dive right into this colorful fish snack!

Ingredients for one:
1 slice of sandwich bread
tinted milk
soft butter or margarine
1 chocolate chip

Utensils and supplies:
3 plastic bowls
red, yellow, and blue food coloring
fish-shaped cookie cutter
new, thin paintbrushes
toaster
1 plastic knife per child
napkins

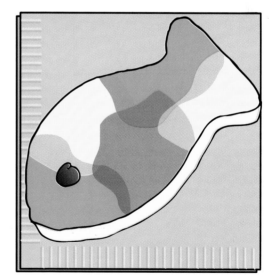

Teacher preparation:
- Pour one cup of milk into each of three plastic bowls.
- Use food coloring to tint one bowl of milk red, one yellow, and one blue.
- Put a new, thin paintbrush in each bowl of milk.
- Arrange the ingredients and supplies near the step-by-step direction cards.
- Assist students with the toaster as needed.

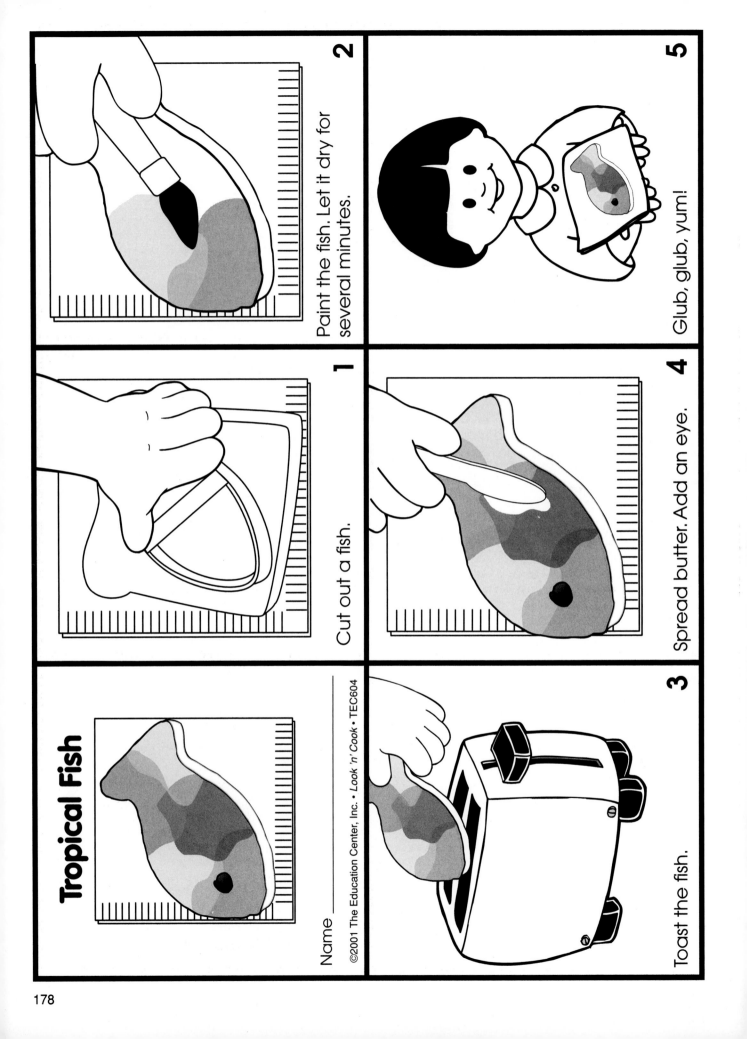

Tropical Fish

Name _____

1 Cut out a fish.

2 Paint the fish. Let it dry for several minutes.

3 Toast the fish.

4 Spread butter. Add an eye.

5 Glub, glub, yum!

Tropical Fish

2 Paint the fish. Let it dry for several minutes.

5 Glub, glub, yum!

1 Cut out a fish.

4 Spread butter. Add an eye.

3 Toast the fish.

Tropical Fish

Glub, glub! Your youngster will be bubbling with enthusiasm as we make tasty, colorful fish treats! To help us with this cooking project, please send in the item indicated below by _____. Thanks for making your child's learning fun and exciting!

___ loaf of sandwich bread

___ tub of soft butter or margarine

___ $^1/_2$ gallon of milk

___ bag of milk chocolate chips

___ package of food coloring

___ package of plastic knives

___ package of napkins

I made a **Tropical Fish** in school today!

My favorite part was _____.

It tasted _____.

This is what it looked like:

Chef's signature _____

An extra helping: Check out plenty of tropical fish in the book *Fish Eyes: A Book You Can Count On* by Lois Ehlert.

Summer Pop

Mmm! These cool pops will hit the spot on a hot summer day!

Ingredients for one:
2 tbsp. vanilla yogurt
2 tbsp. crushed pineapple (drained)
2 tsp. frozen orange juice concentrate

Utensils and supplies:
1 3-oz. paper cup per child
permanent marker
bowl
tablespoon
teaspoon
1 craft stick per child
freezer
napkins

Teacher preparation:
- Personalize a cup for each child.
- Allow the juice concentrate to thaw.
- Drain the crushed pineapple; then put it in the bowl.
- Arrange the ingredients and supplies near the step-by-step direction cards.
- Freeze the prepared treats for several hours before serving.

Summer Pop

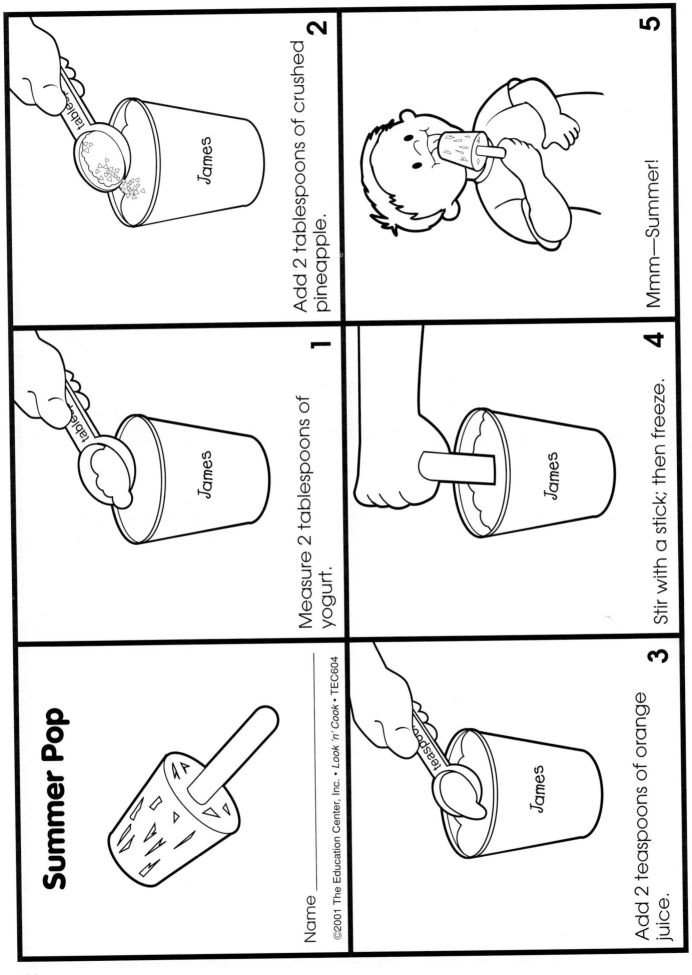

2 Add 2 tablespoons of crushed pineapple.

5 Mmm—Summer!

1 Measure 2 tablespoons of yogurt.

4 Stir with a stick; then freeze.

Name _____

©2001 The Education Center, Inc. • *Look 'n' Cook* • TEC604

3 Add 2 teaspoons of orange juice.

182

Summer Pop

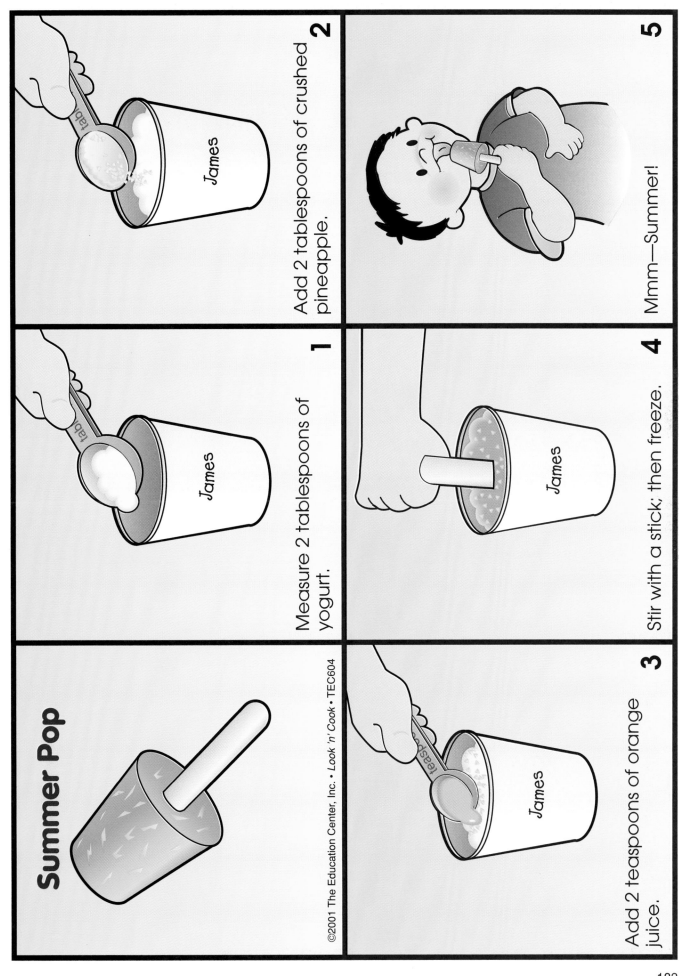

2
Add 2 tablespoons of crushed pineapple.

1
Measure 2 tablespoons of yogurt.

5
Mmm—Summer!

4
Stir with a stick; then freeze.

3
Add 2 teaspoons of orange juice.

©2001 The Education Center, Inc. • *Look 'n' Cook* • TEC604

183

Summer Pop

We will be making tropical fruit pops in school! To help us with this cooking project, please send in the item indicated below by _____. Thanks for making your child's learning fun and exciting!

___ large container of vanilla yogurt

___ large can of crushed pineapple

___ can of frozen orange
    juice concentrate

___ package of 3-oz. paper cups

___ package of napkins

©2001 The Education Center, Inc. • *Look 'n' Cook* • TEC604

I made a **Summer Pop** in school today!

My favorite part was _____.

It tasted _____.

This is what it looked like:

Chef's signature _____

An extra helping: Searching for a delightful summer book to read with your child? Choose *Come a Tide* by George Ella Lyon the next time you visit your local library.

©2001 The Education Center, Inc. • *Look 'n' Cook* • TEC604

Pineapple Upside-Down Cupcake

These miniature upside-down cupcakes will turn your youngsters topsy-turvy!

Ingredients for one:
1 tsp. brown sugar
1 tsp. crushed pineapple (drained)
$1/4$ c. yellow cake batter

Utensils and supplies:
1 foil cupcake liner per child
permanent marker
2 plastic bowls
2 teaspoons
cupcake tins
$1/4$-cup measuring cup
oven
1 paper plate per child
1 plastic spoon per child
napkins

Teacher preparation:
• Personalize a foil cupcake liner for each child.
• Put the brown sugar and a teaspoon in a bowl.
• Drain the crushed pineapple and put it and a teaspoon in a bowl.
• Follow your favorite recipe to prepare yellow cake batter. Refrigerate it until needed.
• Arrange the ingredients and supplies near the step-by-step direction cards.
• Bake the cupcakes in the cupcake tins according to the recipe directions. Let them cool before serving.

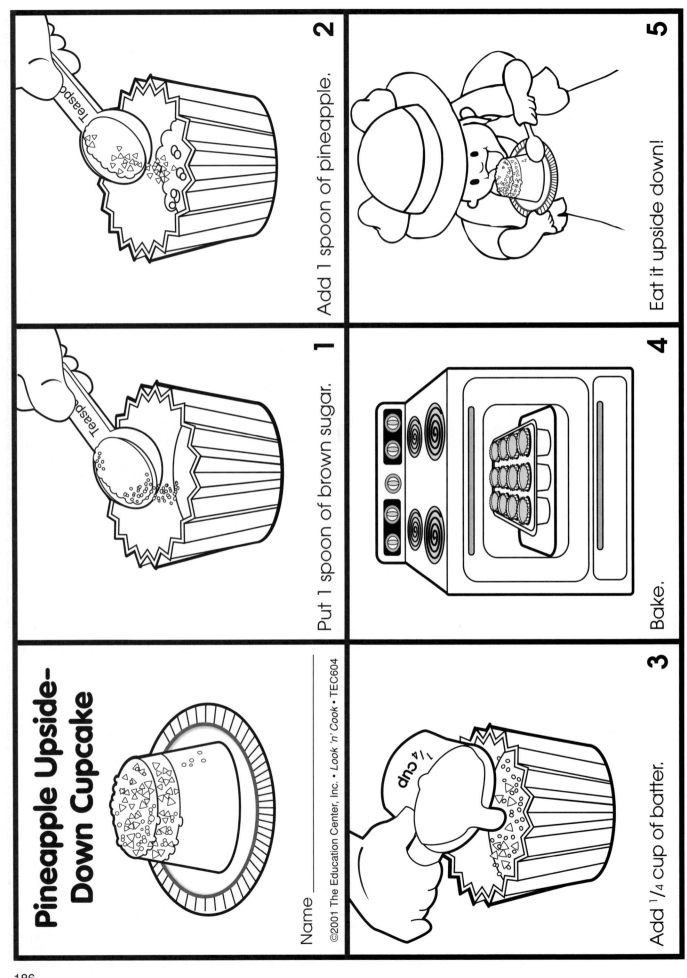

2 Add 1 spoon of pineapple.

5 Eat it upside down!

1 Put 1 spoon of brown sugar.

4 Bake.

Pineapple Upside-Down Cupcake

Name _____

3 Add ¹/₄ cup of batter.

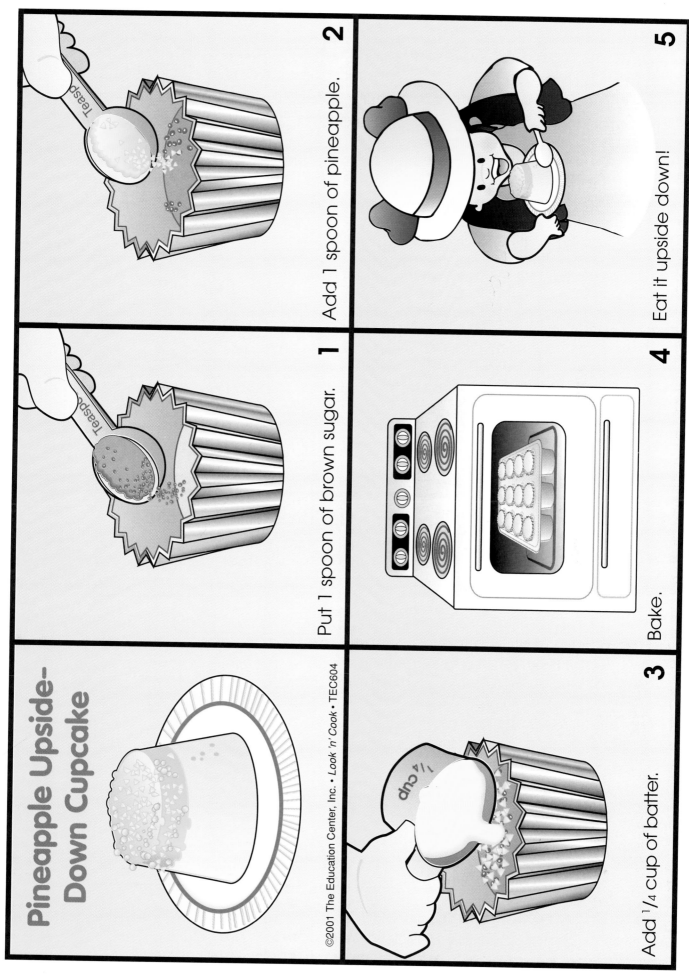

Pineapple Upside-Down Cupcake

2 Add 1 spoon of pineapple.

1 Put 1 spoon of brown sugar.

5 Eat it upside down!

4 Bake.

3 Add ¼ cup of batter.

©2001 The Education Center, Inc. • Look 'n' Cook • TEC604

187

Pineapple Upside-Down Cupcake

Our class is going to be baking miniature pineapple cupcakes for snacktime. To help us with this cooking project, please send in the item indicated below by _____. Thanks for making your child's learning fun and exciting!

___ box or bag of brown sugar

___ large can of crushed pineapple

___ package of foil cupcake liners

___ package of paper plates

___ package of plastic spoons

___ package of napkins

I made a **Pineapple Upside-Down Cupcake** in school today!

My favorite part was _____.

It tasted _____.

This is what it looked like:

Chef's signature _____

An extra helping: Read *The Topsy-Turvies* by Francesca Simon for a silly upside-down story!

Seashell Salad

Sample the seashore with some scrumptious seashell salad!

Ingredients for one:
¹/₃ c. small cooked pasta shells
1 tsp. ranch dressing
1 baby carrot

Utensils and supplies:
large plastic bowl
medium plastic bowl
1 bowl per child
¹/₃-cup measuring cup
1 teaspoon
1 plastic spoon per child
napkins

Teacher preparation:
• Cook, drain, and rinse the pasta; then refrigerate it in the large bowl until needed.
• Pour the ranch dressing into the medium bowl.
• Arrange the ingredients and supplies near the step-by-step direction cards.

Seashell Salad

Name _____

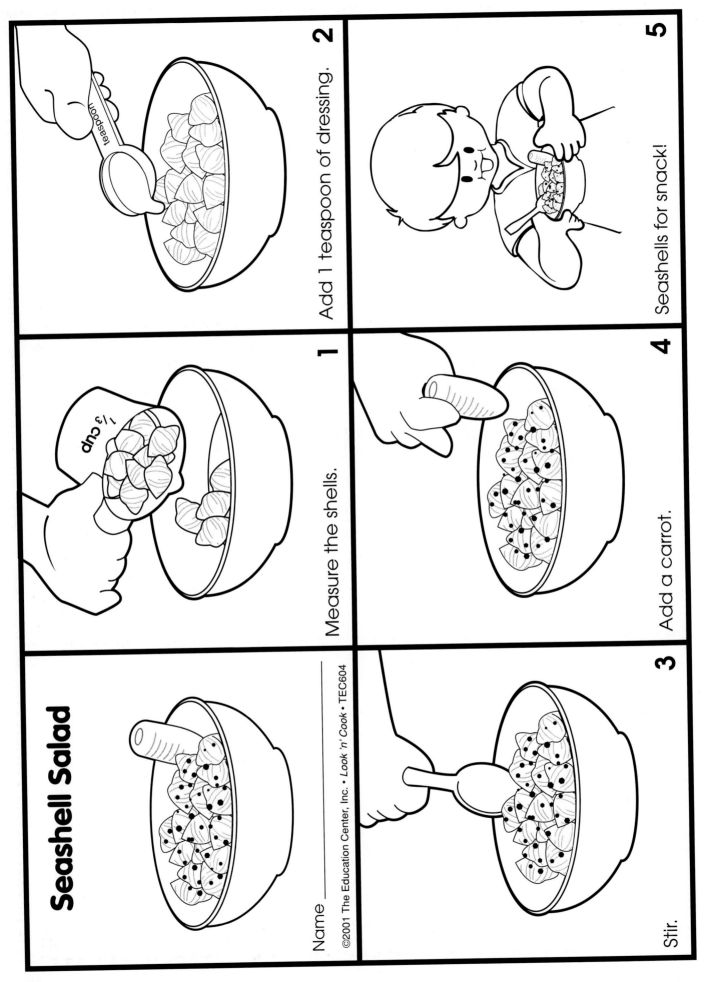

1 Measure the shells.

2 Add 1 teaspoon of dressing.

3 Stir.

4 Add a carrot.

5 Seashells for snack!

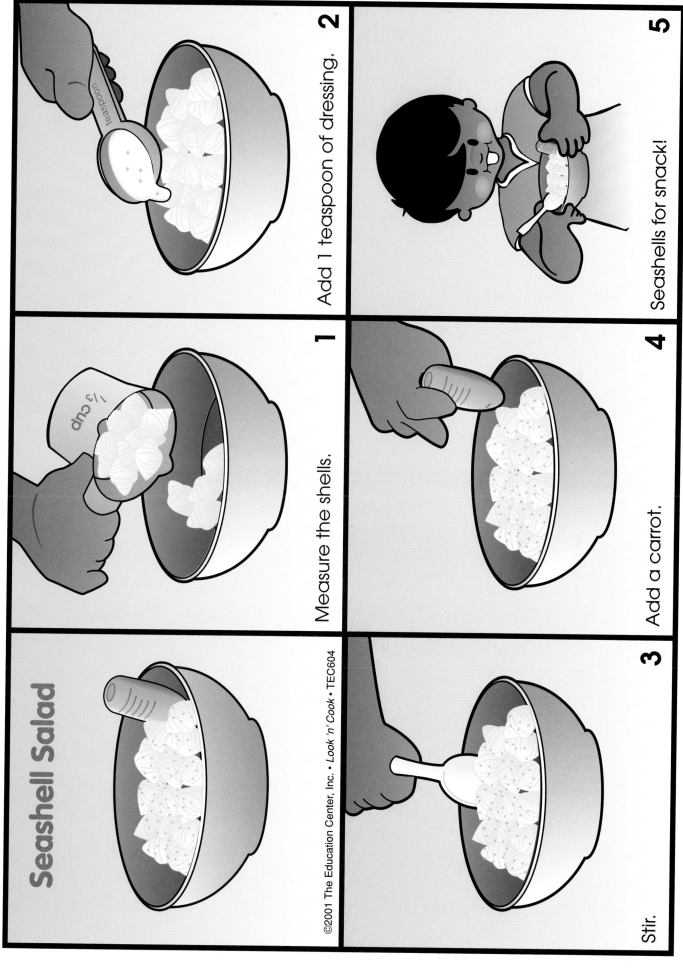

Seashell Salad

2 Add 1 teaspoon of dressing.

5 Seashells for snack!

1 Measure the shells.

4 Add a carrot.

3 Stir.

©2001 The Education Center, Inc. • *Look 'n' Cook* • TEC604

191

Seashell Salad

Surf's up! In our classroom, we're going to follow simple directions to make a nutritious salad! To help with this cooking project, please send in the item indicated below by _____. Thanks for making your child's learning fun and exciting!

___ package of small uncooked pasta shells

___ bottle of ranch dressing

___ bag of baby carrots

___ package of disposable bowls

___ package of plastic spoons

___ package of napkins

I made a **Seashell Salad** in school today!

My favorite part was _____.

It tasted _____.

This is what it looked like:

Chef's signature _____

An extra helping: On your next trip to the library, look up *A Summery Saturday Morning* by Margaret Mahy. Summer has never been more fun!